# African Islam

# AFRICAN

by René A. Bravmann

# ISLAM

Co-published by
Smithsonian Institution Press
and
Ethnographica
1983

First published in 1983 by
The Smithsonian Institution Press
Washington DC 20560, USA
and simultaneously by
Ethnographica Ltd
19 Westbourne Road,
London N7 8AN, Great Britain

Library of Congress Cataloging in Publication Data

Bravmann, René A.
  African Islam.

  Bibliography: pp. 119-120
  1. Islam–Africa, Sub-Saharan. I. Title.
BP64.A1B69   1983      297'.0967      83-20174
ISBN 0-87474-282-X
ISBN 0-87474-281-1 (pbk.)

Designed by Stuart Hamilton/Ethnographica
Typeset by TNR Productions, London
Printed in Great Britain by BAS Printers, Over Wallop, Hampshire

# Contents

# Preface

This selection of essays and the exhibition it accompanies explore some of the social and historical dynamics as well as the aesthetic response of Africans to the appearance of Islam south of the Mediterranean littoral.

Through the avenues of trade and holy wars, Islam had an impact on a significant portion of African thought, life, and art. In particular, craft specializations and aesthetic sensibilities closely followed the spread of the faith in East and West Africa, across the Sahara, spreading throughout the Sahel and encroaching upon the forest zone. Newly introduced objects, forms and techniques found a place in traditional pre-Islamic cultures, at times replacing figurative arts, at other times existing side-by-side or fusing old and new into syncretic forms that share aspects of both cultures.

Dr René A. Bravmann, Guest Curator and author of this book, has focused upon his personal experiences with Islamic thought and art. His essay conveys a sense of the artistic richness, the complexity of pattern, and the delicacy and directness of design that permeates Islamic artistic traditions. His text serves as an introduction to this seriously neglected area of African studies.

In addition to Dr Bravmann, we would like to acknowledge the contributions of those members of the staff of the National Museum of African Art, Smithsonian Institution, who were closely concerned with the exhibition: Lydia Puccinelli and Roslyn Walker of the Curatorial staff, Bryna Freyer of Archives, and Caroline Michels of Exhibition Design.

Finally, neither the exhibition nor this essay would have been possible without the cooperation of museums and private collectors who have lent objects and furnished photographs. Our debt to them is cited throughout the catalogue; our thanks to them for their generosity.

Sylvia Williams, Director
Roy Sieber, Associate Director

# Acknowledgements

I was in Marrakesh in August 1982, carrying out research on the Sudannic elements in this remarkable city, when I received a letter from Jean Salan of the National Museum of African Art, Smithsonian Institution, asking if I would consider curating an exhibition for the museum on the arts of African Islam. Flattered, I responded with a cautious yes and said that we should discuss this project upon my return from Morocco in September. The exhibition was in fact conceived in late November when I met with Mr John Reinhardt, then Acting Director of the Museum, Jean Salan and various members of the staff in Washington, D.C. Although fully aware of the fact that we were on a very tight schedule, since the exhibition would have to open in November 1983, we decided that it could be accomplished if everyone worked together as closely as possible. I want to take this opportunity to express my deepest thanks to the many people who contributed their time, thoughts and energy to make this exhibition and publication a reality. Without their encouragement and cooperation this surely could never have been achieved.

Enid Schildkrout, Belinda Kaye, Evelyn Feld and Carolyn Lasar of the American Museum of Natural History; Diana Fane and Carol Parlato of the Brooklyn Museum; Kate Ezra and Susan Vogel, Metropolitan Museum of Art – the Michael Rockefeller Memorial Collection; Helmut Nickel and David Alexander of the Arms and Armour Collection of the Metropolitan Museum; Leon Siroto; Philip Schuyler; Leland and Barbara Morgan; Paula Ben-Amos, University Museum, University of Pennsylvania; Ron Barber and Edward Grusheski, Museum of the Philadelphia Civic Center; Frederick Lamp, Baltimore Museum of Art; Philip Lewis, Field Museum of Natural History; Margaret and Henry Drewal; John Paden; Ivor Wilks; John O. Hunwick; Justine Cordwell; John W. Nunley, St. Louis Museum of Art; Tom Seligman and Kathy Berrin of the M.H. De Young Museum; William Siegmann; Judith Bettelheim; Barbara Busch and Frank Norick of the Lowie Museum of Anthropology (University of California, Berkeley); Doran Ross, Museum of Cultural History (U.C.L.A.); Arnold Rubin; Grace Johnson, San Diego Museum of Man; Edward Rogers and Valerie Grant of the Royal Ontario Museum; Jane Victor of the De Menil Foundation; Robin Poyner; Norma Wolff; William Hommel; Pam McClosky and Norman Skougstad of the Seattle Art Museum; David Spain; Carol Eastman; Seyed Muhammad Maulana; Eugene C. Burt; Labelle Prussin; Jere Bacharach; Irene Bierman; Samuel Sarick; Ernie Wolfe III; Sarah Brett-Smith; Blake Robinson. I also want to express my thanks to the many private collectors who generously contributed objects to this exhibition.

The advice and consistent help of several colleagues have been extremely important; these people include Farhat Ziadeh, Simon Ottenberg, Ray Silverman and John O. Hunwick. A special note of thanks is due to Malcolm McLeod of the Museum of Mankind, British Museum, and Francine N'Diaye of the Musée de l'Homme, who responded to my urgent letters of request with speed and wisdom. Stuart Hamilton, managing editor of Ethnographica, helped me through the final stages of the manuscript when I most fully needed and appreciated his patience and wit. Over the years many Muslim friends and informants have served as my mentors, and it is their thoughts and beliefs that lie at the heart of *African Islam*.

Without the encouragement and support of the National Museum of African Art and its staff this project would have been inconceivable. I am deeply indebted to Sylvia Williams, who inherited *African Islam* and assumed responsibility for it with grace and cheer. Roy Sieber's timely arrival at the museum helped to lend clarity and focus to the exhibition. Bryna Freyer was able to acquire exhibition photographs in what seemed world record time. Roslyn Walker, Lydia Puccinelli, Caroline Michels, Holly Laffoon, Jean Salan, Janet Stanley, Ed Lifschitz, Joan Saverino, Emily Dyer, Alicia Taylor, Amina Dickerson, Maggie Bertin, and others, too numerous to mention, all contributed to *African Islam* – an excursion into the artistry and character of belief.

To my children Paul and Rachel, who endured this past spring and summer while my mind was on leave and otherwise preoccupied, I have returned. My wife, Stevie, has been a part of all this from the beginning, and her critical insights, sensibility and loving support are evident everywhere.

René Bravmann, November 1983

# Illustration credits

René Bravmann: plate no. 52, CI, CII; The trustees of the British Museum: plate no. 34; The Brooklyn Museum: plate nos. 29, 44, 87; Diane Cooke: plate no. 21; Field Museum of Natural History: plate nos. 12, 17, 40, 45, 70; Fine Arts Museums of San Francisco: plate no. 30; Hickey and Robertson, Houston: plate no. 46; Indianapolis Museum of Art (and Robert Wallace, photographer): plate no. 64; Jesper Kirknaes: plate no. 3; Lowie Museum of Anthropology, University of California, Berkeley: plate nos. 41, 56, 57, 65; Metropolitan Museum of Art, New York: plate nos. 33, 35, 69, 76; Professor J.C. Moughtin: page 6; Musée de l'Homme, Paris: Plate nos. 32, 61; Museum of the Philadelphia Civic Center: plate nos. 67, 74, 80, 81, 85; National Museum of African Art, Smithsonian Institution: plate no. 78; and Asman Photo: front cover, p. 14 and plate nos. 4, 15, 18, 22, 24, 25, 26, 27, 58, 59, 63, 68, CIII; and Eliot Elisofon (photographer): plate nos. 28, 43, 49, CIV; and Delmar Lipp (photographer): plate nos. 48, 79; Robert Nooter: plate no. 82; John W. Nunley: plate no. 60; Royal Ontario Museum: plate nos. 38, 55; Seattle Art Museum: plate nos. 47, 51; William Seigman: plate no. 16; Raymond A. Silverman: plate nos. 13, 14; UCLA Museum of Cultural History (and Richard Todd, photographer): plate nos. 1, 36, 37, 42, 50, 62, 66, 72, 75; University Museum, University of Pennsylvania: plate nos. 31, 73; University of Washington, Seattle: plate nos. 2, 11; Sarah Wells: plate nos. 6, 7, 8, 9, 10, 19, 39, 71, 77, 83; Rob Wilson: title spread; Barbara Wise: plate CIVb. Plates 53 and 54 are taken from *Divertissements de Kong* by M. Prouteaux, Bulletin du Comité d'Etudes Historiques et Scientifiques de l'Afrique Occidentale Française, 8 (4), 1925.

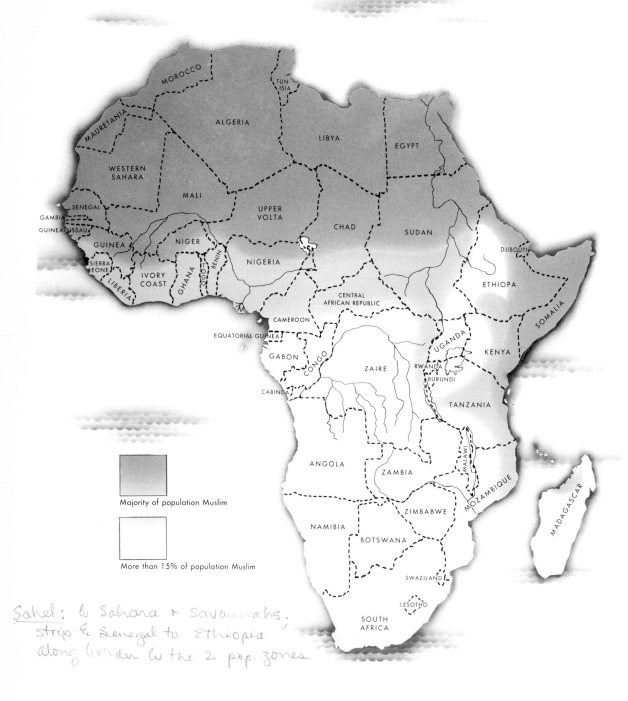

MOROCCO

TUN ISIA

ALGERIA

LIBYA

EGYPT

WESTERN SAHARA

MAURETANIA

MALI

SENEGAL

GAMBIA

GUINEA BISSAU

GUINEA

NIGER

UPPER VOLTA

CHAD

SUDAN

DJIBOUTI

SIERRA LEONE

LIBERIA

IVORY COAST

GHANA

TOGO

BENIN

NIGERIA

ETHIOPA

CENTRAL AFRICAN REPUBLIC

CAMEROON

SOMALIA

EQUATORIAL GUINEA

GABON

CONGO

ZAIRE

UGANDA

KENYA

RWANDA

BURUNDI

CABINDA

TANZANIA

ANGOLA

ZAMBIA

MALAWI

MOZAMBIQUE

ZIMBABWE

NAMIBIA

BOTSWANA

SWAZILAND

LESOTHO

SOUTH AFRICA

MADAGASCAR

Majority of population Muslim

More than 15% of population Muslim

Sahel: b/ Sahara + Savannahs.
strip fr Senegal to Ethiopia
along border b/ the 2 pop. zones

# Introduction

There has been, in the West, a resurgence of interest in things Islamic that is quite remarkable. This interest is due, in large part, to the fact that Islam has begun to impress itself upon our political consciousness and is representative of a series of economic forces that affect us all. Emanating from this set of concerns has been an attempt to elucidate the creativity of Islamic civilization and to render its achievements visible to the public. Through a number of major, and some more modest, exhibitions museums are anxious to exhibit their Islamic holdings: one grand exhibition, 'The Heritage of Islam,' has been touring the United States for the past two years and has been attracting unusually large audiences.

It is within this climate that *African Islam* was conceived. The administration and staff of the National Museum of African Art, Smithsonian Institution, felt that the moment was particularly ripe for an exhibition devoted exclusively to the arts of African Islam. The focus of this effort was to be upon Saharan and tropical Africa instead of upon the urban and Muslim North African areas invariably honoured in general exhibitions of Islamic art. For me the exhibition represented a fresh opportunity to look broadly at a long ignored portion of Islamic civilization, at a religious culture that has profoundly influenced much of Africa, and to explore certain dimensions of this faith and its creativity.

The monuments and artistry of this enormous region (equivalent in size to the Near and Middle East and India), have never really concerned the art historians of Islam for they have been too far removed from the centres of the Muslim world and shaped, as it were, at the extreme edge of this civilization. Regarded as provincial and peripheral, as apprehending a very different reality, these arts remain an eternal other – they exist but go unnoticed and unattended. *African Islam* was, therefore, designed to demonstrate that the arts of this vast area of Africa belong fully within the Islamic orbit. They are a testament to the remarkable diversity of mind and sensibility found within Islamic civilization, and they are, for me, among its most vital and unique expressions.

*African Islam* is essentially a set of personal reflections about this religious culture and Africa that stem from over 15 years of observations, experiences, and lessons learned from many Muslim friends and informants living in Ghana, Ivory Coast, Upper Volta, and Senegal. For the purposes of this exhibition and catalogue I have suggested certain themes that strike me as particularly important if one is attempting to begin to comprehend the breadth and nature of this religion and its artistry.

Islam in Africa is nearly as old as the faith itself for within a generation of the death of Muhammad (d. 632 AD) Arab soldiers were already in Alexandria and by the end of the century had effectively moved across the rest of North Africa to the very northern border of present day Mauretania. Military campaigns and conversion went hand in hand and ancient Berber populations in Morocco, Algeria, and Tunisia were gradually converted to the faith.

In the ninth century the recently Islamized Berbers carried the religion into the Sahara, to places like Sijilmasa in southern Morocco and Murzuk in the Fezzan, where Islam was to eventually gain these important Saharan trading towns. Parts of the eastern Sudan, the Horn, and the east coast of Africa were also affected during this early phase of Islamic expansion although in these instances it was not conquest but Arab commercial enterprise that led to the introduction of the religion. Trade was crucial and these regions became nominal parts of the Umayyad Caliphate, with its capital at Baghdad, in the late seventh century. Yemenite and Arab traders established a number of trading communities along the Eritrean and Somali shores and inaugurated a tradition of intensive commerce between the Arabian peninsula and the Horn and eastern Africa that continues to this day.

From these auspicious beginnings along the edge of the continent, Islam moved slowly and inexorably into Africa. Conversion of the Sanhaja Berbers propelled Islam fully into the western Sahara among the Sarakholle (Mande speakers also known as Soninke) in Mauretania. By the end of the tenth century Sarakholle converts had already pushed into the Senegal River valley and as far as the Niger River where their religious zeal touched the important regions of Takrur and Massina. A less dramatic but even surer advance of the faith occurred along the trans-Saharan trade routes dominated by the Islamized Berbers and Tuaregs and between the tenth and seventeenth centuries every major Sudannic state from Senegal to the upper Nile (Ghana, Mali, Songhai, the early Hausa states, Kanem-Bornu, Wadai, and Darfur) whose ascendency was to a great extent based upon control of these commercial arteries, was affected by the presence of Islam. Local political and economic institutions took on a Muslim cast and much of life itself, including the arts and architecture, assumed some of the trappings of Islam. The religion also had a decided influence upon the intellectual life of many of these kingdoms and cities like Timbuktu, Gao, and Kano became centres of considerable Islamic learning. Muslim leaders such as Mansa Musa of Mali, Askia Muhammad of Songhai, and Idris Alooma of Bornu (whose deeds are kept alive even today by praise singers and authors), were known through northern Africa and in the Near East.

These Sudannic states were an important part of the vast economic empire created by Islam and their influence was also felt further south, in the forest region of West Africa. Dyula and Hausa Muslim traders from some of these states carried not only the products of the Sudan and of the trans-Saharan trade but also brought Islam into what are today the countries of Guinea, Sierra Leone, Liberia, Ivory Coast, Ghana, Togo, Benin, Nigeria and Cameroon.

The progress of Islam on the eastern side of the continent also continued although it was far less dramatic and always much more confined in terms of its geographical impact. In the eastern Sudan Arab settlement was restricted to the Red Sea shore from Suakin to the Danakil coast and it was not until the sixteenth century, with the gradual decline of Christian Nubia and Ethiopia, that Arab and Iraqi teachers and mystics were able to outflank these kingdoms and carry Islam into the upper Nile valley. These efforts proved especially effective in the Kingdom of Sennar and later in Darfur. Despite several attempts to gain a foothold in the Ethiopian highlands, Muslim efforts were finally repulsed in the sixteenth century and thereafter

Islam remained a purely coastal phenomenon. Nowhere was the coastal nature of Islamic influence more obvious than around the Horn of Africa and along the East African coast from modern-day Kenya to the northern border of Mozambique. Along this entire coastal strip Arab and Persian traders and clerics created a remarkable series of Islamic trading towns and city-states – Berbera, Mogadishu, Merca, Brava, Malindi, Mombasa, Zanzibar – where Somali/Arab and, further south, Swahili cultures flourished and were nourished by contacts with Arabia, the Persian Gulf, and western India.

After nearly a thousand years Islam had come to influence much of Africa north of the Equatorial forest and east of the great Rift Valley. While increasingly affected by the political and religious prestige and economic power of the faith, however, African Muslims did not assume the role of passive recipients of Islam but shaped the religion whenever necessary to fit local circumstances: a synthesis developed between the universalistic orientation of Islam and traditional beliefs and perceptions that proved vital and enduring.

It was against this historical backdrop, and the mounting threat of European colonialism, that the history of African Islam entered a new phase. The nineteenth century is filled with the names of Muslim leaders, religious reformers, and militant nationalists who sought to purify and reinvigorate Islam and stem the tides of European encroachment. Among the former surely the most famous was the Fulani social reformer and mystic Usuman dan Fodio, whose jihad or holy war against the Hausa States was to permanently change the political face and tenor of Islamic life in northern Nigeria. Of the militant resistors the careers of Al Hajj Umar, the Mahdi Muhammad Ahmad, and Muhammad Abdallah Hasan are remarkable for their unbending resistance to European force and their efforts to establish new political entities based upon Islamic principles.

The turbulence of the nineteenth century did little to slow the growth of Islam and it may be argued that from this experience the faith became stronger and a more potent political force. Even during the colonial period when certain European powers, particularly the French and Portuguese, regarded Islam as a potential threat, the religion continued to expand its influence. This was certainly the case in British and German territories where Muslims and their culture were often admired and where they were allowed to direct their affairs in relative freedom. In many areas Islamic religious orders played a crucial role in fostering the sentiments of nationalism, as was the case with the revival of the Mahdiya in the Anglo-Egyptian Sudan, or in further promoting Islam by encouraging its teachers and mystics to carry its message into new regions such as Uganda and the interior of East Africa.

The influence of Islam continues unabated today, answering the needs of its adherants throughout much of the continent. That it has forged a special relationship with its believers, that Islam and Africa have made something of each other that is quite extraordinary, lies at the heart of *African Islam*.                                                                R.B.

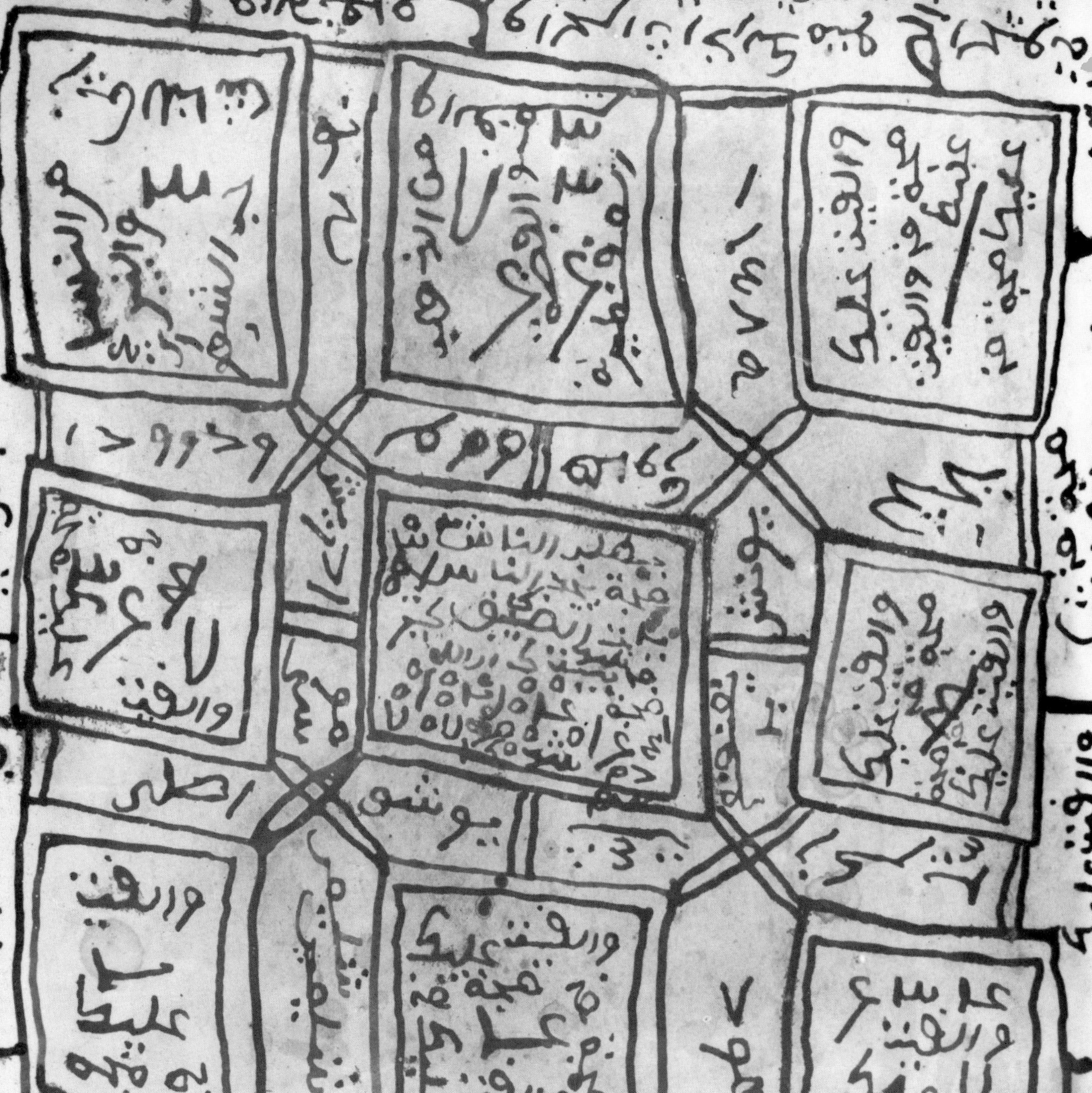

stems from the deepest of sources, a medium whose affective power is far greater than ordinary speech.

Geertz alerts us to the fact that it is not only within the realm of oral poetry, and of course of religion, that the language of God is invoked, but within daily discourse as well, for 'ordinary conversation is laced with Qurannic formulae to the point that even the most mundane subjects seem set in a sacred frame'.[3] The sounds and phrases of Allah imbue language and life with a special tonality that conveys the passion for the words of God so audible and visible in Saharan and tropical African Islamic life.

My initial exposure to the beauty and potency of the Koran and its language, and to the fact that it is, to use Geertz's words, 'the vehicle of a divine message', a 'holy object',[4] came within a few days of my first visit to Africa. My wife and I had just arrived in Ghana and were settling into student life at the University in Legon when we were visited by a trader, a Muslim from Katsina in Nigeria. Hearing that we were Americans new to Legon he stopped at our verandah, probably from a mixture of curiosity and a desire to trade. His name was Abdallah and when he realized that we were not potential clients, we began a long and animated conversation. His command of English was considerable and he treated us to stories of his trading ventures, photographs of his wives and children and his opinions on a wide range of topics. Abdallah was an enormously appealing and engaging man, physically imposing in his large and lavishly embroidered full-length blue gown and with a sharpness of mind and wit that was striking. He exuded self-confidence and I sensed that here was a man who would surely feel at ease in any situation.

We had talked for much of the afternoon when Abdallah's body suddenly stiffened and a look of consternation filled his eyes. He stood up abruptly, mumbled somewhat incoherently about the lateness of the hour and asked to be excused. Picking up a carefully rolled grass mat and an old tin kettle, the only items within his large bundle of goods that he had not displayed for us, he moved away quickly and stopped under the shade of a nearby mango tree. Abdallah filled his kettle at a stand-pipe near the edge of the compound, carefully washed his hands and feet, and then thoroughly rinsed out his mouth. Returning to the tree he unrolled his mat, pinning its corners securely to the ground with stones, and stepped out of his sandals onto the mat.

Facing east, towards Mecca, this worldly and self-confident man began an intimate conversation with God. Abdallah's powerful voice softened, yet his words sounded stronger, as if they issued not from his mouth but from somewhere deep within him. I heard him call Allah's name and then repeat what I took to be short prayers and invocations. No matter where his phrases led him he always came back faithfully to God. Abdallah's words and body were directed solely towards Allah, they were meant for him alone, but his words carried so easily that they filled the space between us. The force of his phrasing and intonation were such that his words seemed to defy the laws of sound – they remained suspended in the air and I could hear and appreciate their clear beauty. His body, wiry and strong, moved with the rhythms of his verse; from an upright position he inclined his

1

upper torso towards his God, or kneeled, hands upon his thighs, sitting upon his heels. Whether seated or standing, he moved his head gently forward or tipped it to the right or left. His hands, held openly and gracefully, emphasized the flowing movements of his entire body. He used them to cup his ears and support his full prostrations, or held them before his eyes as if they were sacred tablets.[5] Abdallah's mat and four stones were his religious precinct, all he needed to shut out the world about him and to enter into personal discourse with Allah. He later told us that Abdallah

2

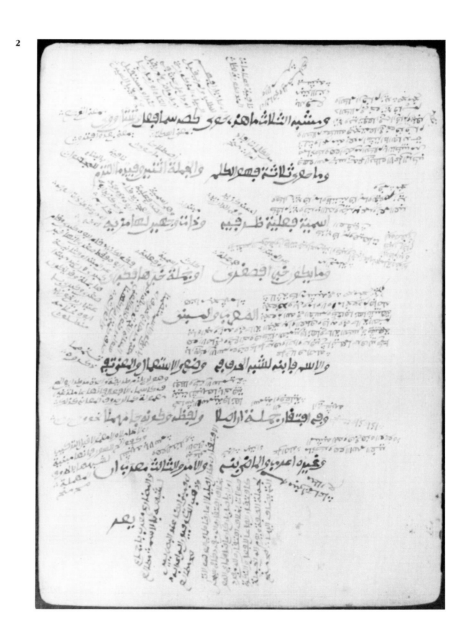

meant 'servant of Allah'; we had experienced this man living his name.

I learned a great deal from watching Abdallah that afternoon. He introduced me to the rudiments of the daily prayers, *salat*, as performed by a most committed Muslim. He also exposed me to something far deeper – the extraordinary power of Allah's language. Abdallah's prayer had come from the heart, and the beauty and potency of the verse transformed him from a worldly trader into a humble man of God. Allah must have surely heard him.

We saw quite a lot of Abdallah in the following weeks. He seemed genuinely to enjoy the company of students and visited us regularly. It soon became apparent that there was a special closeness between this man and his God: the name Allah, phrases invoking Allah, variations upon his name and apt references from the Koran punctuated his thoughts and speech. Greetings, departures, the sharing of a meal, a cool drink, or the news of the day seemed to call for an invocation of God's name. Allah, in one form or another, prefaced or served to conclude much of what our new friend had to say: the topic under consideration seemed to make little difference; it mattered not at all whether the subject was serious or trivial, Abdallah rarely strayed far from his master. At the time I thought this dependence on God rather curious and somewhat obsessive. I understood the importance Abdallah attached to daily prayer, since it is regarded as one of the basic requirements of his faith, but I was totally unprepared for what appeared to be God's invasion of his very being. What I failed to appreciate was that God had not imposed his will upon Abdallah, but that Abdallah had invited God to permeate his life.

Since then I have met others like this Muslim from Katsina – some more learned, others less so – who have shared a similar passion for the words of God. I have also come to know certain places, Muslim communities ranging from small rural villages to large, sophisticated urban centres, that have seemed to be steeped in much the same feeling. In such places the sounds of God mingle just as easily with the local languages like Dyula, Bobo and Wolof as they had with Abdallah's conversational English. Within these Muslim settings the public call to prayer five times a day is almost inescapable, its rhythmic repetition a recurrent feature of life, but what is most insistent and enduring is that same passion for the words of God. His words are constantly upon the believer's tongue –within the market-place, the privacy of home, or in the most casual of conversations on the streets. They are the sounds that remain in one's ears, as persistent and palpable as any Islamic monument to the eye. For believers there is indeed a potent acoustic quality to God's omnipresence.

The faithful not only feel and hear Allah's presence about them, they can actually see and touch it, for African Muslims transform the words of God, this passion for His sound, into clear and immutable shapes. African aesthetic sensibility merges everywhere with the literary and graphic potential of Islam, bringing a particular stability and form to God's words. African Islam, an old and vital blend of religion and culture, calls upon the skills of its scribes and scholars, as well as the cunning of its artists, to make visible God's presence in this world.

**2**

An Arabic manuscript from Nupe country consisting of (part 1) a treatise on prosody 'The Unique Concerning Grammar, Syntax and Calligraphy' by al-Suyuti (d. 1505) and (part 2) 'The Poem of al-Khazraji'. The copyist was Muhammad al-Badmasi and it was written in Egga and the town of Bida. Nupe, Nigeria. Paper, ink. 21.5 cm Collection of John O. Hunwick

One encounters everywhere in Muslim Africa examples of these transformations of Allah's language but before turning my attention to them I want to consider a particular work that should help to clarify what I mean. The object, a woven mat of natural and dyed grasses, is a stunning example of Swahili weaving and to my mind surely one of the treasures of the Tanzania National Museum (Plate 3). Woven in the village of Moa, near the important coastal town of Tanga in northern Tanzania, it exhibits all the love for geometric pattern generally found in Swahili *mswala* or prayer mats.[6] Yet what distinguishes this *mswala* from others (including the finely woven example from the Museum of the Philadelphia Civic Center on page 107) is that the

rhythms of geometry are framed and banded by God's words. Somehow, almost miraculously, the artist managed to weave into this 'place of prayer' (the literal meaning of the word *mswala*) what appears to be classical Swahili verse rendered in Arabic characters. The script occurs within five narrow bands that run virtually the full length of the mat and in another band around its border, and is punctuated at regular intervals by the stirring invocation 'In the name of God', known to all Muslims as the *bismillah*. Allah's praise name, *Karamallah* or 'God the beneficent', also occurs at several points throughout the weaving and a single reference to the Prophet – 'Muhamadi Muhutari Nabiya' or 'Muhammad the Chosen Prophet' – is found in the very centre of the mat.[7] The verses themselves are somewhat more difficult to decipher for, according to Seyed Muhammad Maulana, a native of Mombasa, Kenya, they appear to be executed in a very localized script. What one cannot fail to appreciate, however, is that the weaver from Moa, using the humblest of materials, literally wove his passion for God and the prophet into a 'place of prayer.'

**3**

References to Allah's praise name 'Karamallah', and to Muhammad the Chosen Prophet 'Muhamadi Muhutari Nabiya', are woven into this Swahili prayer mat (*mswala*) from Moa, in northern Tanzania.
Natural and dyed grasses.
Tanzania National Museum Collection.

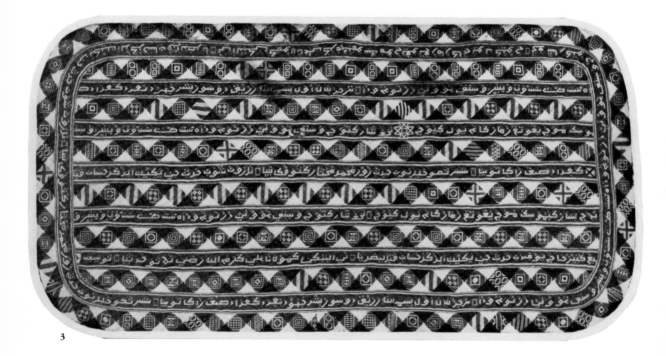

3

**4**

Prayer beads are a most visible example of the passion for the words of God. Rich ebony beads, beautified with silver wire inlay, remind the faithful of their obligations to Allah — the daily prayers — and the efficacy inherent in the repetition of His name.

Moor, Mauretania. Silver, ebony. 34 cm
Private Collection, Washington, D.C.

**5**

Written in a splendid, angular Hausa/Bornu script, this copy of the Koran is enhanced with exquisite marginalia, a common feature found in copies of the Holy Book.

Hausa, Nigeria. Paper, coloured inks, tooled leather. 23 cm
Department of Anthropology, National Museum of Natural History, Smithsonian Institution. #341.636

**4**

**5**

Many objects demonstrate the desire of Muslims in Africa to transform the flux of sacred language, Koranic Arabic (which as we have seen has its own special potency and acoustic properties) into fixed configurations of the divine, but I shall confine my discussion to a select few in order to explore the richness of these transformations. I shall begin with a work that most emphatically expresses God's place among his believers, a splendid leather-bound text in the Morgan Collection acquired in the important Tuareg city of Agades in Niger. Written in an elegant, angular Bornu-Hausa script and richly illuminated with figures of God's creatures, including a frog and ostrich, a variety of magical squares and signs and lovely calligraphic designs in the margins of the text, it is a particularly fine example of a personal volume owned by a wealthy and pious Tuareg man (Plates 6 and 8). Encased in a tooled leather pouch and suspended on a thong it was worn publicly as a conspicuous pendant, with the enclosed text resting just below the owner's heart.

Such a book is referred to in the Tuareg language Tamashek as a *tcherot*, or amulet, and while the work is a popular West African Islamic divination manual, the *Kitab Moussa* or *Book of Moses*, it is replete with references to God's majesty.[8] Allah occurs everywhere, either invoked directly by name or elliptically through cryptic letters and numbers. Beyond these multiple reminders of God there is a glorious page consisting of a painted spiral with the Koranic verse (*Sura* 2: 256) known as the *Ayat al Kursi* (the 'Throne Verse') written within its contours (Plate 7):

God
there is no god but He, the
Living, the Everlasting.
Slumber seizes Him not, neither sleep;
to Him belongs
all that is in the heavens and the earth.
Who is there that shall intercede with Him
save by His leave?
He knows what lies before them
and what is after them,
and they comprehend not anything of His knowledge
save such as He wills.
His Throne comprises the heavens and earth;
the preserving of them oppresses Him not;
He is the All-high, the All-glorious.[9]

**6**

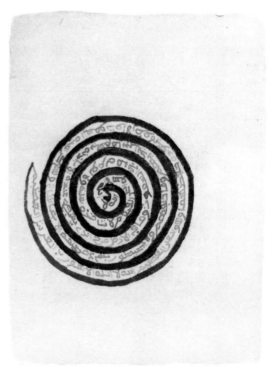

**7**

The *Ayat al Kursi*, one of the most beautiful passages in the Koran, is a poetic assertion that this divination text, indeed its very efficacy, is entirely dependent upon God's will. Its verse stirs the soul, a sublime statement of Allah's all-encompassing nature and omnipotence.

**6, 8**

Two representations of God's creatures, a frog and ostrich, from a copy of the *Kitab Moussa* or Book of Moses, a popular West African divination manual. This leather-bound text was worn as a large pendant by a pious Tuareg man.
Tuareg. Agades, Niger. Paper and coloured inks, 12.5 cm
Collection of Leland and Barbara Morgan

**7, 9**

Painted spiral with the Ayat al-Kursi written within its contours. This sublime Koranic verse, Sura 2: 256, describes Allah's encompassing nature and His omnipotence. Another page from the Tuareg Tcherot (amulet) is seen in Plate 9.
Tuareg. Agades, Niger. Paper and coloured inks, 12.5 cm
Collection of Leland and Barbara Morgan

**10**

There are indeed many ways of presenting visually one's passion for God, and African artists are masters at exploring them. Delicate jewellery, a fan meant more for protection than comfort, and large textiles with brightly-painted shapes and writing all attest to man's desire for closeness to Allah. A small and finely-shaped silver pendant from Omdurman, Republic of Sudan, asserts belief through five different praises of Allah and the Prophet, each skilfully inscribed within the four petals and centre of a carefully rendered flower (Plate 10). They are, beginning in the centre and moving clockwise from the top around the pendant – 'Praise be to God', 'In the name of God the merciful', 'Blessing is to the Prophet', 'God's name is his will' and 'I depend upon God'.

**11**

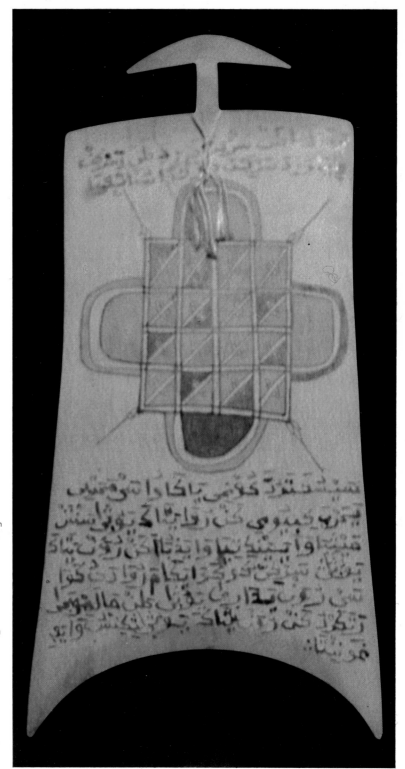

**10**

A small silver pendant with praises of Allah and the Prophet delicately inscribed within the four petals and centre of a flower.

Omdurman, Republic of Sudan. Silver 8 cm
Collection of Leland and Barbara Morgan

**11**

Pyro-engraved Kanuri calabash with depictions of Koranic boards that evoke the presence of Allah and the efficacy of the holy word amidst the images of modernization — aeroplanes, trucks, etc.

Kanuri, Nigeria. Gourd. 50 cm
David Spain

**CI**

A Koranic prayer board with Northern knot and magic square.

Hausa, Nigeria. Wood and coloured inks, 48 cm
Collection of John and Karen Paden

see Art of the Arab World (Atil), p 11 for explanation of prayer board format (tabula ansata = tablet with a handle)

12

**12 and CII (detail)**

Collected in northern Togoland at the
turn of the century, by Captain Thierry,
a German Colonial administrator, this
prestige fan includes numerous
references to one of Allah's 99 names,
*Ya Hafiz* – 'Oh Protector' or 'Oh
Guardian' – along its outer edge.
Hausa (?). Togo. Wood, paper, coloured inks.
102 cm
Field Museum of Natural History. #104.941

Paper, cloth, wood and coloured inks are combined in a nineteenth-century (Hausa?) fan collected by Captain Thierry, a German colonial
administrator stationed at the important trading
centre of Sansanne Mango in northern Togo, and
acquired by the Field Museum in Chicago in 1905.
Along the entire outer edge of the fan are multiple
references to one of Allah's ninety-nine names, 'Ya
Hafiz', meaning 'Oh Protector' or 'Oh Guardian',
while the inner band includes the phrase 'May God
protect and preserve you . . .'. Held by someone of
high rank it displays dramatically God's shielding
presence (Plate 12).

A man may drape himself in a cloth covered with colourful squares and endless repetitions of Allah, swathing his body in God's name, as in an example from the Bono state of Techiman in central Ghana.[11] Made in 1980 by Al Hajji Abdullahi Muhammad, Imam of Techiman, it was inspired by the words and illuminations of a local manuscript version of the *Dalail al Khiryat*, 'The Proofs of Excellence', written by the famous fifteenth-century Moroccan Berber mystic, Al Jazuli. Brilliant and sparkling squares of colour (magenta, blue, orange and yellow) applied with a brush establish a vibrant grid for the cloth, but what is most remarkable is the name 'Allah' written in the interstices between the

**13**

**13**

Al Hajji Abdullahi Muhammad painting the 'Muslim Cloth' using the words and illuminations from a local copy of the *Dalail al Khiryat* written by the fifteenth-century Moroccan Berber mystic al-Jazuli. (See Plate 15.)

**14**

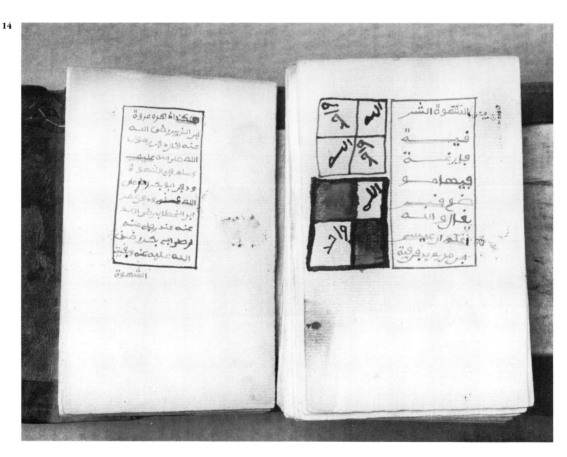

squares and elsewhere. This textile is full of God's presence, like the sounds in a community of his believers, but perhaps its most perfect analogue is the endless repetitions of Allah's name that suffuse the grand litanies of the Sufi brotherhoods of West Africa, especially in the Friday night services of the Tijanniya order, whose members chant Allah's name a thousand times or more in order to achieve a oneness with the Divine.[12] In the Imam's cloth God is encoded – the name Allah is reduced to two or three vertical strokes written from right to left and followed by a small circle or dot, but it is fully sufficient and recognizable as an apt expression of the Divine. (Plate 15).

**14**

A Ghanaian copy of the *Dalail al Khiryat*. This classic text is particularly important among the Muslim Mande where it is read at the funerals of prominent men and during many of the holiest days of the religious calendar.
Techiman, Ghana. Paper, coloured inks, leather. 25 cm
Collection of Raymond A. Silverman

**15**

A cotton cloth, painted with colourful squares and endless repetitions of the name of Allah, made by Al Hajji Abdullahi Muhammad, Imam of Techiman, in 1980.
Techiman, Ghana. Cotton, water colours. 245 cm
Collection of Raymond A. Silverman

15

**16**

Falui masquerader at Kenema, an important Mende town in Sierra Leone. More recent Falui have leather or cloth-wrapped Koranic charms sewn at intervals along the length of the conical head-dress.      Photograph taken by William Siegmann at Kenema in 1973

God's sounds are indeed ubiquitous. Incapable of being confined, they may be heard and seen in the most remarkable places. Two Mende masks from Sierra Leone, one a Falui or Yoma Yoma head-dress, the other an entire life size costume (*Goboi*) collected in the chiefdom of Bumpe in the 1920s are compelling examples of this fact.[13] The first consists of imported cloth and raffia, embroidered with cowrie shells and crowned by rich purple and black feathers. It has six wooden tablets with what appear to be Arabic words painted upon them. The second combines an abundance of grass, blue and white striped cotton cloth, patches of red, black and white homespun, mirrors, cowries, goatskin, goat's hair and fifty-four miniature Koranic tablets with script. Both are impressive masked beings, highly public manifestations directed and controlled by men, but apparently independent of the pre-eminent male masking society, the Poro, that so dominates Mende culture.[14] Entertainers of a high order, they integrate a variety of colours and shapes that cannot fail to please their audience. But what ultimately fascinates the eye are all the Koranic tablets, some strung like a sacred fillet about the base of Falui's head-dress, the others carried almost penitentially in the mantle worn on the back of the *goboi*. Sheer love of Arabic lettering highlights the six tablets about the head of Falui, for they are not readable, but the dramatic proclamation 'Ya Allah', 'Oh God', clearly reverberates from the heavy load of *goboi's* Koranic boards trailing along the dancer's back. So it is among the Mende, in a world where Allah and African creativity surely meet and mingle, along frontiers marked by the blending of belief and imagination.

**17**

A Mende Falui head-dress (called Yoma Yoma by Mandingo speakers) embroidered with cowries, crowned by feathers, and encircled by a fillet of 6 wooden tablets with pseudo-Arabic script painted upon them.

Mende, Sierra Leone. Cloth, wood, shells, feathers. 19 cm
Field Museum of Natural History, Chicago. #220853

بسم الله الرحمن الرحيم اللهم صل على
سيدنا محمد وعلى ال محمد وسلم

اللهم صل على محمد وسلم

# CHAPTER TWO

# God's Secrets – shaped in silence

'One doesn't leave a friend at a crossroad', said Didier as we set out late one evening to see a well-known marabout, a Muslim seer possessed of formidable healing powers and ability to forecast the future.[1] I had been in Bobo-Dioulasso, in Upper Volta, barely a month in the summer of 1982, and in less than a week I would be leaving the comfort of friends and the familiarity of this city for eight weeks' research in Marrakesh, Morocco. This was an exciting prospect, yet I was increasingly anxious about my journey. Didier, a close friend and constant companion during that month, was concerned for my well-being and had arranged for me to meet this holy man (whom I will call Mamadou) for he was certain that he would be able to help. 'I think you're simply afraid of the unknown', he kept repeating, 'but Mamadou understands God's secrets'.

Didier was not a Muslim. A teacher at a local *lycée*, he was known throughout Bobo-Dioulasso as a free-thinker and an eccentric. Fiercely independent, but an excellent and popular teacher, he had achieved a position of respect in the city. He was outspoken and at odds with most members of his family, yet he often sought out Mamadou and had developed an unshakeable confidence in the man. 'You will not only see but you will feel his sincerity', he said, as we made our way to Mamadou's house on the outskirts of the city. 'He is very secretive, but he has a pure heart.'

Arriving at Mamadou's home we were met by his wife, a slight and nervously energetic woman who was tending a cooking fire in the middle of the compound. She offered us each a stool by the fire while we waited to see her husband. Wanting to know more about this man, I asked Didier why he was so certain that Mamadou could help curb my fears. Didier's faith in the marabout was, he said, based upon a number of facts that he had learned about him over the years. Mamadou's heritage, he said, was remarkable. His mother came from a famous family of Dafing hunters, a people known in this part of the country for their power and courage. From his father Mamadou had inherited the collective wisdom of an important Peul or Fulani lineage of Muslim scholars and teachers.

Born and raised in Wahabu, a noted centre of Islamic learning since the early nineteenth century, Mamadou was the privileged son of two impressive intellectual traditions. From his maternal grandfather he had learned the secrets of the natural world as only hunters, and especially Dafing hunters, know them. From his father and other learned men of Wahabu he received a thorough grounding in Islam, not only in the esoteric and literal dimensions of the faith, *zahir* (the study of the Koran, the commentaries upon the holy book and exegesis), but its inner aspects, or *batin.* Mamadou had devoted much of his time to learning the mystical properties of Arabic words, numbers and letters and this had given him a firm foundation for understanding the hidden faces of God. Didier had come to respect Mamadou's deep learning, but even more important to my friend was the man's character. Mamadou used his extraordinary know-ledge wisely and morally and had a high degree of empathy for, and sensitivity to, others. 'The man rarely says a word, he is always listening – he hears not only with his ears but with his heart', said Didier.

**19** An old woman, moving painfully with the aid of a cane, emerged from Mamadou's room and his wife signalled that we could enter. I followed Didier and stepped carefully over the threshold and down a single step into the room. Mamadou's chamber was warm, dark and intimate, and as my vision adjusted to the dim light issuing from one small kerosene lamp, I saw an elderly man clad in white sitting cross-legged on a mat in the farthest corner of the room. He looked frail, insignificant even, as if totally dominated by his surroundings. The place was full of things –books, papers, animal skulls, old jars etc filled with various substances – they were Mamadou's secrets and they loomed all about him. He greeted us in a soft voice and pointed to two leather cushions, where we sat in silence for what felt a long time. Mamadou's eyes were constantly upon me, and I felt both uncomfortable and touched by the warmth of his gaze.

Didier broke the stillness by telling Mamadou why he had brought me and something of my history; a summary that included my reasons for being in Bobo-Dioulasso, words about my family and about our friendship. The marabout said nothing, but listened and kept me within his sight. When Didier had finished, Mamadou turned slowly towards the wall and gathered together a number of items that were within easy reach: a hawk's beak; six eggs (four of which were covered with black and red signs); a Koranic board that gleamed from repeated use; a small mirror held within a frame of brightly-painted flowers; eight cowrie shells; two gourd bowls, (each filled partially with water), and a worn and yellowed Arabic manuscript.

Mamadou turned back towards us and assembling this collection of objects before him began a long and complex journey into the mysteries of his craft. He cast the cowries again and again, noting their configurations with pen and ink upon the board. Spreading sand upon his mat, he carefully aligned the eggs in patterns that seemed to correspond to those created by the shells. The mirror had been placed in such a manner that it reflected every detail of this complex procedure. Mamadou held the hawk's beak between the middle fingers of his left hand and used it to mark **20** a certain rhythmn on the lips of the gourds. Three times he opened the Arabic manuscript at specific places and nodded, apparently satisfied that each selection related well to everything else.

He worked intently and openly, yet I understood little of what was happening. Towards the end of the session he turned his back to us again and after many minutes faced Didier and presented him with a small vial of dark liquid and what appeared to be a rectangular packet wrapped in cotton thread. He spoke rapidly, giving him a set of instructions that he was to convey to me after our departure. Finally, Didier told me that Mamadou had finished. I placed a small gift on the mat, we thanked him and prepared to leave. The marabout took my hands tenderly, looked into my eyes and murmured what I took to be a prayer.

We said nothing on the way back to Didier's house, and it was only after we had arrived that either of us felt the urge to talk. Didier began by conveying Mamadou's instructions in detail. I was to have the amulet, *sebe*, wrapped in leather the very next day and was to wear or carry it until I had finished my work in Morocco. No one, not my closest friend nor my wife, was to know about it. The vial contained a special solution called *nassa-ji*, a wash that Mamadou had made from the words and marks placed on his Koranic board. I was to rub a small amount of it on my chest or place a drop on my tongue whenever I felt uncertain or afraid. Mamadou had told Didier that these were now my secrets and if I treated them carefully nothing could possibly happen to me. A rather sceptical person by nature, I nevertheless took the vial and amulet and followed Mamadou's instructions in the weeks ahead.

Surprised by my own acceptance of what had happened and full of questions, I stayed with Didier and we talked about the marabout and his powers until daybreak. As we talked I realized that Mamadou's appeal and power seemed to stem not only from his abilities to manipulate and marshall a host of forces, but from the fact that he knew and understood completely the strong and necessary relationship between silence and secrecy. He was well versed in the occult, but there were others with such knowledge. What separated Mamadou from other ritual experts was his ability to see through people while remaining impenetrable himself. It seemed that his self-enforced silence inspired confidence in him and was the key to his strength and influence over people. Certainly I was deeply affected by Mamadou's silence earlier that evening. It had made the few words he had spoken much more intense, and his slightest gesture more commanding.

**21**

A superb Tuareg copper amulet with the phrase 'Oh God, bless our master Muhammad and give him peace' inscribed at the top. The many squares, of magical significance, appear to be numbers and letters based upon the Tuareg script *Tifinar*.
Dr. Brett-Smith

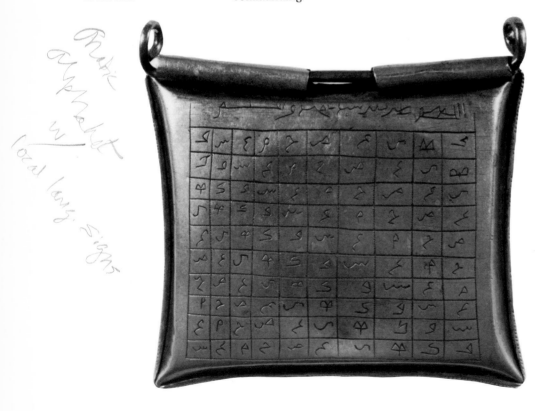

Mamadou indeed conceived and shaped his secrets in silence, but as Didier suspected they most likely derived their ultimate force from the marabout's closeness to God. Mamadou, in a rare moment, had once confided to Didier that while he used many materials in his work, some obtained from certain shrubs and plants, others from the animal world, at the core of all his secrets were the words of Allah. These words he knew well: they came not only from the Koran and religious texts, but from a number of treatises on magic, divination and numerology that he had either inherited directly or copied by hand from his father's library. To be able to read and write God's language, his very words, was particularly important, for it allowed Mamadou to exercise through his mind and pen a continual claim upon the Divine. His ability to concentrate God's words in writing, to give shape and form to sacred language, allowed him access to extraordinary powers and these he had long used skilfully and with considerable prudence.

Mamadou was not only quiet and discreet, he guarded his secrets well. According to Didier he was not the kind of marabout who engaged in selling his knowledge, a rather common practice according to my friend. His library was his private domain, where he carried out his consultations and slept. On those few occasions when he left the library, he carefully locked the room. No one was permitted entry in his absence. Mamadou carefully guarded not only his books but the very words, signs and drawings within them, for they formed the basis of his powerful amulets. How he selected and manipulated these magical elements, one could only imagine, but this was another part of his secret and prompted an even greater silence on his part. Writing was his medium, that special tool critical to his work, and by its very nature perfectly suited to him for it further encouraged him to operate in almost perfect silence. His amulets and the processes by which he devised them remained in his mind and heart, the private property of a deeply informed imagination and belief.

**22**

An elaborate necklace consisting of large imitation amber beads which are strung to a metal amulet case (known as *herizi*) with wire inlay and adorned with small bells. It contains either a Koranic verse, a magic square, or part of a Cabbalistic text.

Somalia. Amber-like beads, base metal and fibre. 26.5 cm
National Museum of African Art, Smithsonian Institution, gift of John L. and Katheryne Loughran. #76-16-1

Didier and Mamadou taught me to see and appreciate the environment of silence and secrecy within which amulets are conceived. Silence and secrecy, however, are important not only in the making of amulets but are central to their existence as objects of power. The range of charms created by Muslims in Africa, the variety of their shapes and the materials employed in their creation is breath-taking, yet all amulets are alike in that they are concealed truths. Whether written on paper and covered with leather or encased in metal, or a liquid suspension kept in a vial or carved container, such as the *nassa-ji* prepared for me by Mamadou, amulets are nearly always shielded from the public eye and kept within the shadows of culture.[2] The owner of an amulet is the keeper of potent knowledge based upon carefully arranged and organized secrets, and thus someone who possesses a particular treasure that cannot be known or shared by anyone else.

**23**

Rotated squares and flowering circles grace these two Mandingo amulets that are man-made reflections of the order and perfection of Allah's creation.
Mandingo, Liberia. Dyed leather, metal and paper. 9.5 cm
National Museum of Natural History, Smithsonian Institution. #168083

**24**

Somali silver amulet with agate beads. Agate is used by many peoples of the Horn of Africa in the making of jewellery and amulets because of its strong protective and medicinal qualities.
Somalia. Silver, agate, fibre. 20 cm
National Museum of African Art, Smithsonian Institution. Gift of John L. and Katheryne Loughran. #76-16-3

23

24

African Islamic charms, regardless of their outward form or intended purpose, appear to be composed of two parts – a written portion and a design or graphic element. Edmond Doutté, in his classic work *Magie et Religion dans l'Afrique du Nord*, refers to these two elements as the *da'wa*, or 'spell', and *jadwal*, or 'picture'. Some amulets include only a *da'wa*, others only a *jadwal* with little or no writing, but many are glorious and creative works combining the strengths of both elements. The *da'wa* may derive from a number of Islamic sources including the Koran (surely the single most important reference), astrological treatises and divination manuals or books on numerology; the *jadwal* may be based upon magical squares, images of the planets and their movements, or an impressive variety of geometic configurations.[3]

Charms are made by the learned and by those who have had minimal instruction. Both groups find substantial theological support within Islam for their magical practices. The field of magic is complex, as E.W. Lane noted in his study of Islam in Egypt, and Muslims readily distinguish between divine or spiritual magic, *Er-Roohanee*, and a natural or deceptive form known as *Es-Seemiya*. *Er-Roohanee* derives its strength and affective power from its alliance with God and operates through his legions – the angels, the good jinn, the prophets – all those cosmic forces aligned with him. It is practised by men of good will who employ the secret names of God and his miracles for positive ends. Those who deal within the realm of *Es-Seemiya*, however, carry out their craft with a closed heart, depending upon 'perfumes and drugs', the deceivers of man.[4]

The words and pictures found inside amulets, like those which are written and drawn upon Koranic tablets and then washed off to make 'writing water', lie at the very heart of these secret charms. Each is an ardent demonstration that African Muslims seek in God's words and signs a pathway to his immanence and majesty. To utilize Arabic, Allah's language, is to attempt to draw upon God himself in order to shape one's destiny within this world. Writing and drawing in such instances are not only inherently powerful, tangible forces, but are mediated by the manipulative and analytic capacities of the human mind.[5] Doutté's words regarding this aspect of written charms make the point nicely:

> In the first place you can carry them around, put them wherever you wish, then divide them, write them in different ways, on the spot, backwards: a great number of amulets are written in boustrophedon (like a plow moving in alternate directions), reputed to have a most magical character. Moreover, the words of a single formula can be separated, aligned in series, distributed according to various geometric designs; in this way words belonging to different classes of ideas could be mixed. For example, the names of God, the names of angels, the names of demons, verses of the Quran, are scattered in geometric figures, laid out in squares, broken down into letters . . .[6]

Islamic amulets serve as vivid reminders that while man needs Allah he must invest his dependence upon God with reason and creativity. These charms are undeniably representations of the rationality within magic.

23

**25**

A large amulet made by Alfa Diallo, a
Fula Koranic teacher from Timbo in the
Futa Jallon highlands of Guinea, at
Bafodea, Sierra Leone. A particularly
powerful charm, it was used as a
model for making other amulets. The
names Allah and Muhammad occupy
the centre.

Fula, Sierra Leone. Coloured inks, graph paper.
52 cm
Collection of Simon Ottenberg

**26**

God's secrets are elegantly enclosed in
a silver case worn as a pendant by a
pious Tuareg. Geometric designs based
upon the square, and its rotation and
reflection, add touches of visual delight
to this personal object.

Tuareg, Mali. Silver, fibre. 43 cm
Collection of Mr. and Mrs. E. David Harrison

A particularly splendid example of the explicit combination of the rational and magical elements of Islamic amulets was obtained by Simon Ottenberg in 1980 in Bafodea Town, in the Limba country of northern Sierra Leone. Generously proportioned, the charm is nearly square, with 52 cm sides, drawn in red, black and purple inks on graph paper. Arabic, written in a script known as Maghrebi Kufic, covers much of both sides of this large amulet and is conspicuously confined within the various boldly coloured square and rectangular patterns that dominate its overall design (Plate 25). Known locally as a *hatumere*, the name commonly used to designate all Muslim charms in this region, it was obtained from Alfa Diallo, a Muslim Fula from Guinea who was resident in Bafodea Town and earned his living as a maker of amulets and a teacher.[7]

According to Ottenberg, Alfa Diallo received this *hatumere* from his teacher, Amadu Wure Diallo of Timbo, an important Fula (or Fulbe) centre of Islamic learning approximately 130 km. north of

Bafodea Town in the Futa Jallon highlands of Guinea.[8] Diallo's teacher had received the *hatumere* from his own *karamoko* years before and thus this particular amulet, because of its age and pedigree, was regarded as especially powerful.[9]

Alfa Diallo used this *hatumere* as a model, a guide for the making of other amulets, for he felt its efficacy derived from the fact that it was a potent composite of various portions of the Koran. The many charms which he copied from the model included only small segments of it, and were generally written on paper, soaked in water, and then used by their new owners as a special solution (*nassi*) with which to wash themselves as protection against the attacks of witches and to bring good fortune. While the names Allah and Muhammad occupy the very centre of the amulet and other Koranic references do appear in this *hatumere*, a significant portion of the writing consists of esoteric formulae and signs. Indeed an important book of Sudannic authorship entitled *A Treatise on the Magical Use of the Letters of the Alphabet* may well have inspired this amulet for it has long been a popular magical manual in West Africa[10] Written by Muhammed b. Muhammad al-Fulani al-Kashinawi, an early eighteenth-century Fulani scholar and mystic from Katsina in Northern Nigeria, it is one of seven works attributed to him and devoted to the subject of astrology, numerology and the magical sciences of Islam in general.[11]

Al-Kashinawi continues to be regarded as the single most important Sudannic author on the occult. A deeply religious man, he performed the pilgrimage to Mecca in about 1730 and resided in Cairo, where he continued to deepen his knowledge under the tutelage of the famous Egyptian historian, al-Jabarti.[12] Al-Kashinawi's writings also owe much to even earlier North African devotees of the mystical sciences, including al-Buni, al-Ghazzali and al-Suyuti; thus this amulet may be seen as the result of an impressive international tradition of education devoted to understanding and interpreting the secrets of God.[13] The magical words and signs in this *hatumere*, possibly deriving from al-Kashinawi's treatise, revolve around the power of God's mystical names and enjoin the owner to hold fast to this knowledge, for only through secrecy can one reap the blessings of Allah.

26

27

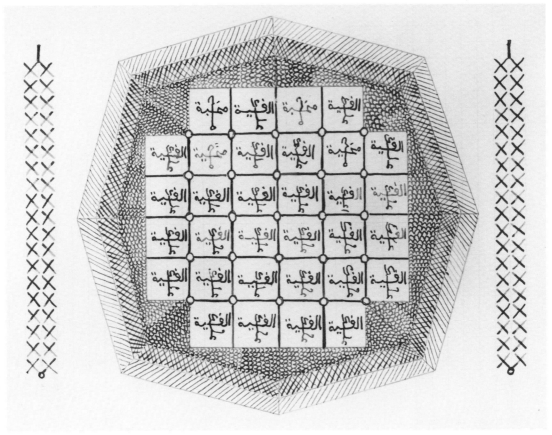

Another fascinating amulet acquired by Ottenberg (although a recent copy of an older example) further demonstrates the African Muslim penchant for shaping the mystical through the organizing powers of the human mind. It is a *hatumere* called *yawa dudu* and was made by Sori Sawaneh, a Limba Alfa from Kamanda, a large town on the northern edge of Bafodea Chiefdom, very near the border of Guinea. According to Alfa Sawaneh, *yawa dudu* is an Arabic phrase meaning 'to guide, or protect, the house' and this charm is a particularly effective deterrent against witches, whom the Limba feel and believe are the root cause of illness and other misfortunes. He learned the secrets of *yawa dudu* from his teacher, a Mandingo cleric at Boke in Guinea, who revealed it to him over a period of intensive study that lasted nearly eight years. Alfa Sawaneh's comments regarding this *hatumere* are interesting, and what follows is the essence of an interview that Ottenberg conducted with him.

The overall octagonal shape of the charm, divided into 32 squares, is essentially a design that encloses the written words and not a drawing of a house and many rooms as the name *Yawa Dudu* might suggest. The red circles connecting the black squares that encompass the Arabic writing merely serve to highlight the corners of the squares where they touch each other. If witches come from any direction and approach the writing they will be overcome and destroyed. The writing, in fact, can only be read by angels and remains utterly confusing and incomprehensible to witches.[14] (Plate 27).

According to Sawaneh the words in the square at the upper right hand corner of the *yawa dudu* are 'Walakaiti Alayhi', that in the square to its left 'Muhibatu', and they come from the Koran. 'Walakaiti Alayhi' is repeated twenty-eight times, 'Muhibatu' occurs in only four squares, and this proportion is apparently maintained in all *yawa dudu*.

What intrigues me about this interview is its

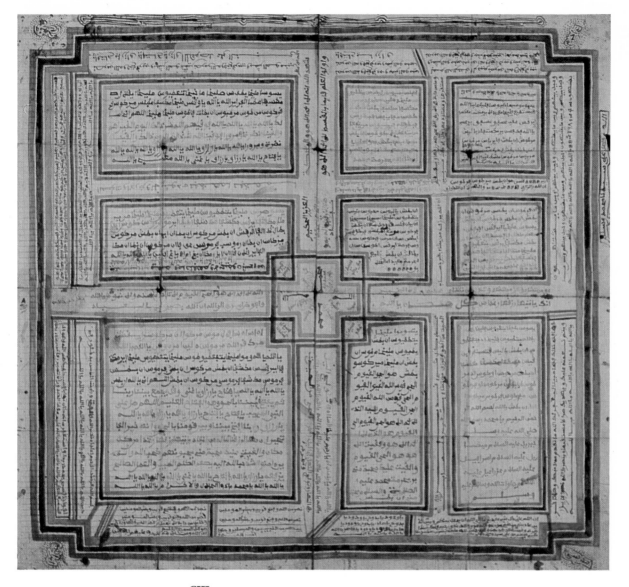

**CIII**

The large amulet made by Alfa Diallo at Bafodea,
Sierra Leone. See also plate 25.

**27**

This amulet, known as *yawa dudu*, means 'to guide
or protect the house'. Made by Alfa Sawaneh, a
Limba from Bafodea, Sierra Leone, it is a powerful
deterrent against the ravages of witchcraft. It
incorporates words from Sura 20 of the Koran, the
powerful chapter of the Holy Book known as Tā Hā.
Limba/Fula. Sierra Leone. Coloured inks and graph paper.
34 cm
Collection of Simon Ottenberg

## CIV

**a**

A Yoruba beaded doll (perhaps an *Egungun* masquerade accessory) reveals the presence of Islam by the large leather amulet it wears.
Yoruba, Nigeria. Wood, coloured beads. 31.7 cm
Collection of Dr. and Mrs. Ernst Anspach

**b**

Two sides of an *omolangidi* doll display the public and secret faces of Islam. Eight Koranic boards appear on one side, while the doll wears a triangular amulet (*tira*) on the other.
Margaret and Henry Drewal suggest that an *omolangidi* may be used as a child's toy or to help a woman conceive.
Yoruba, Abeokuta, Nigeria. Wood. 20.3 cm
Collection of Dorothy Brill-Robbins

guarded generosity. Approached by an anthropologist with considerable professional skill and an ease of manner that can be disarming, Alfa Sawaneh revealed very few details about the *yawa dudu* and maintained a decided reticence regarding its deeper meaning. A true understanding of this amulet remains with him alone. I do believe, however, that if we keep Alfa Sawaneh's comments in mind while examining this amulet more closely, its very words and shapes will help us towards a fuller appreciation of its meaning. To begin with, the words within the squares are instructive, for as John Hunwick informs me they come from Sura 20 of the Koran, the chapter known as *Tā Hā*, and are a part of verse 39.[15] This is how Hunwick deciphers the two phrases that appear throughout the amulet:

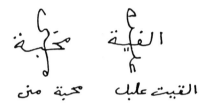

love from me          I shed upon thee

By uncrossing the words within the squares their sense is revealed to the uninitiated: Allah's abundant love conferred upon the possessor of the *yawa dudu* is the surest antidote against the ravages of sorcery. That Alfa Sawaneh selected these phrases from the Sura *Tā Hā* is important, for despite the potency attributed to all Koranic verses, there are some like the *Tā Hā* which are particularly highly regarded and used repeatedly in the making of amulets. This is due not only to the basic content of these suras, which stress Allah's closeness to his believers, but also because each of these chapters (there being twenty-nine in all) begins with a set of mystical letters that are said to be understood only by God. *Tā Hā* ('T' and 'H') are two of these fourteen letters referred to as *mutashabih* and they remain a lingering mystery to the Muslim mind.[16] It is, then, the ultimate mystery of *Tā Hā* that imbues the *yawa dudu* with its particular potency – that allows it to exist among men and yet beyond their ultimate comprehension.

The words, now translated, lend clarity to what Alfa Sawaneh had revealed about this *hatumere*. It is God's love that will preserve its owner, that will arrest the flight of witches and throw them into disarray. The two phrases found within the thirty-two squares constitute a last line of mystical defense, for even if witches should breach the double wall of protection suggested by the double border of the octagon that surrounds these squares, they must finally confront the ultimate power of the words of *Tā Hā* and Allah himself. Sawaneh may well have divided these Koranic phrases, placing the words at right angles to each other as he did, to emphasize the greater than normal power of written Arabic when no longer constrained by its unilineal thrust. Intersection of the words not only creates a set of crossroads within each square, a strong defensive manoeuvre, but also directs the letters outwards towards the four cardinal points, suggesting their ability both to protect and attack in all directions.

Still more interesting, perhaps, is Alfa Sawaneh's handling of the grid and squares and the heaviness of the lines and words within the amulet. Fula and Mandingo charms from the Futa Jallon generally display a set of mystical numbers and letters banded by strong geometric contours composed of very thick lines. This is especially true when the signs within refer to malevolent forces such as bad angels and jinn that need to be held in check, and in which instances the lines are more heavily rendered than the signs themselves. In Sawaneh's amulet the relative weight given to line is reversed, God's words are more generously conceived and shaped and appear incapable of being contained in any final sense within the borders that surround them. The numerous red dots, as Sawaneh indicated, do join the squares at their corners but they are also, to my mind and eye, highly reminiscent of the recitation markers found at the end of phrases in handwritten copies of the Koran from Africa. Such marks punctuate the phrasing and rhythms of written verse, clarifying the language held between them. For me, the red dots in this *hatumere* serve a very similar function, signalling pauses that highlight the potency of Allah's words: it is the power of these words, drawn from the Koran, that will ultimately reverberate in the face of witchcraft. This is what Alfa Sawaneh might well have intended.

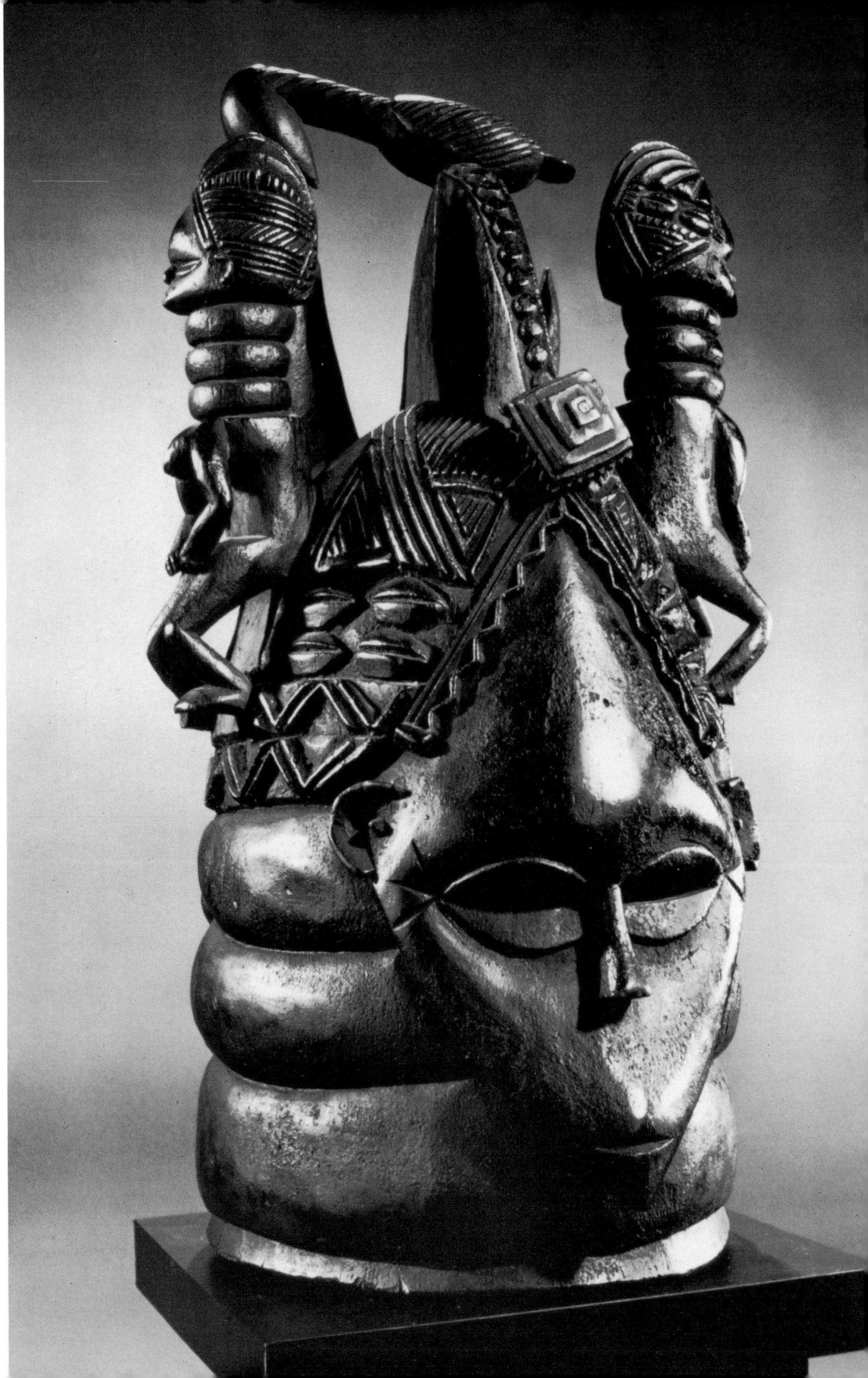

A phenomenon that occurs broadly in Africa, particularly in the continual intercourse between Muslim and non-Muslim life, is the artful blending of one secret with another. I shall look at two examples of Islamic amulets that merge with the secret power of traditional non-Muslim objects, masks, which in themselves are sculptural statements of inscrutible and mysterious forces. The first is a finely carved Sowo mask in the Anspach Collection, executed by a Mende sculptor in Sierre Leone and worn by an elderly woman, a high official, of the female society known as *Sande* (Plate 28). A marvellous example of Sande artistry, it honours *Sowo* the tutelary spirit who is said to guide young girls through the secret steps of initiation into womanhood. I find this mask intriguing, for while surely a statement of ideal female beauty, its calm demeanor also seems to suggest the moral and ethical qualities that the Mende attribute to womanhood. Finely and precisely detailed, it is an eminently readable form, yet it hides within itself untold mysteries, the secrets of Sowo, Sande and the experiences of girls who have been transformed into women. At the top of Sowo's forehead sits a conspicuously carved Islamic amulet referred to by the Mende as Lasimo and this sculpted charm encloses yet another secret, one derived from the mystical world of Islam.[17] Together, Sowo and the Lasimo remind us that we can never fully know what appears before us.

**28**

Sowo, the tutelary spirit of the Sande society, guides young girls into womanhood. The sculpted details of this mask are allusions to Sowo's spiritual and moral qualities, and include a conspicuously carved Islamic amulet (*lasimo*) on the forehead.
Mende, Sierra Leone. Wood, 51 cm
Collection of Dr and Mrs Ernst Anspach

**29**

This Baga shoulder mask dominated by a female form carries a finely incised charm reminiscent of Fulbe craftsmanship.
Baga, Guinea. Wood. 79 cm
The Brooklyn Museum, gift of Mr. and Mrs. John Friede

**29**

30

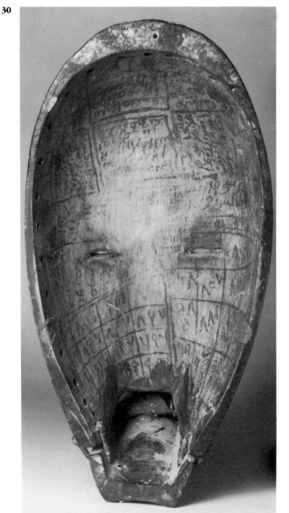

30

In looking at Sowo we have concentrated on the public face of a mask, but Islamic amulets may also be found behind and within masks, as in an example attributed to the Toma of Guinea and apparently used within the male secret society *Poro*.[18] Poro masks, and there are many of them, are manifestations of the spiritual forces behind this brotherhood and serve as guardians of its deepest secrets. The example seen here combines a human face with a powerful beak and thus instantly directs the mind to complex and barely understood notions of transformation. This may be the mask of a senior member of the Poro society, but we cannot be sure. What is more certain, however, is its fixed form, the fact that it most likely represents powerful forces, and that inside the mask, on its inner surface, are drawn many squares that contain the magical letters and numbers of Allah and a cryptic reference to Chapter III of the Koran, entitled 'Palm Fibre' (Plate 31). This short chapter (only five lines long) is also known as the Sura of Abu Lahab (the father of flame) and speaks of one of Muhammad's uncles, the only member of his own clan who opposed the prophet. It is, as noted by Pickthall, 'the only passage in the whole Quran where an opponent of the Prophet is denounced by name'.[19] Sura III is an angry invective hurled specifically at Abu Lahab and his wife, but it is also known as the cursing sura and is generally voiced at moments of betrayal and treachery. Whatever else is expected of this Poro mask, it surely stands as an obdurate sentinel ever ready to defend the organization and its members against treason from within.

**30**

This Mano hornbill mask is a *Poro* spirit with elaborate magical squares, Cabbalistic signs and numbers painted on the inner surface of the face.
Mano, Liberia. Wood, metal, cloth, fibre and ink. 40 cm
Fine Arts Museums of San Francisco. Purchased through the Museum Society Auxiliary

**31**

The inner surface of a *Poro* mask with powerful magical squares, letters, numbers and a reference to Chapter III of the Koran known as the Cursing Sura, or the Sura of Abu Lahab.
Toma, Liberia/Guinea border. Wood, ink. 53 cm
University Museum, University of Pennsylvania #AF 5373

31

32

# CHAPTER THREE

# Victory from Allah – battles waged with words and weapons

In September 1982, in the archives of the Musée de L'Homme in Paris, I happened upon an old photograph entitled 'Trophies of Soliman Ziher', an image that presents yet another dimension of Allah's presence among his believers – the theme of holy war or jihad.[1] (Plate 32) It was in a drawer labelled 'Republic of Sudan', one of several prints headed 'Social Life – Spoils of War'. I was immediately drawn to this curious image of military triumph, of Muslim martial power that was complete and totally dominant; yet the scene had a decidedly stage-set quality about it. It was as if, for the sake of posterity, Soliman Ziher and his soldiers had carefully composed this military tableau after their resounding victory. Three large Muslim banners with Arabic embroidered upon them serve as a monumental backdrop for the captured and dismembered European cannons and mounted guns strewn upon the ground. The flags seem to proclaim the powers of Allah and underscore the utter annihilation of the infidel. Persian scimitars and straight double-edged thrusting swords (kaskaras) are carefully arranged along the sides and above the large central flag, to further emphasize Muslim military prowess. To complete this scene of triumphant Islam are other swords, a number of sheaths, two partially unfurled banners (also embroidered with Arabic and placed diagonally upon the rubble of guns and cannons) and two large side-blown ivory trumpets covered with leopard skin, that would have been sounded during battle to encourage Soliman's legions.

This photograph was one of thousands inherited by the museum in 1937 from the old and poorly documented Trocodero collections, so little was known about it. However, it seems that it had been taken in the late nineteenth century in the Anglo-Egyptian Sudan (what is today essentially the Republic of Sudan); that the name 'R. Budila' in white ink at the bottom of the print was the photographer's; and that Soliman Ziher was probably a commander in the army that followed the Sudanese spiritual leader Muhammad Ahmad, the self-proclaimed Mahdi or Messiah, in his long struggle (1881-95) to resist British and Egyptian rule and establish a state based upon the principles of Islam. Precisely where the photograph had been taken could not be determined, but it seemed certain that it predated the death of the Mahdi in 1895, and was perhaps taken between 1885 and 1893 when the Mahdi's irrepressible forces were defeating the Egyptians and British at virtually every turn.[2]

I purchased a copy of this photograph and my fascination for it has continued to grow. It is not only a vivid reminder of the confrontation between Islam and the British Empire that raged throughout the eastern Sudan at the end of the nineteenth century (bringing to mind the names of the Mahdi, his successor the Khalifa Abdullahi and General Charles George Gordon, as well as the battles of Khartoum and el-Obeid), but for me it expresses the very spirit and reality of holy war.[3] It fully honours the bravery and victory of Soliman Ziher and his followers, yet it is a testament to jihad and the ever-present and guiding spirit of Allah. It commemorates the sacred nature of jihad, an ancient duty as old as Islam itself, that is not only sanctioned in the Koran but was used by Muhammad, in his attempt to spread the boundaries of nascent Islam.[4] Soliman Ziher's war trophies

**32 (title page)**

'The Trophies of Soliman Ziher', a late nineteenth-century photograph. Taken by R. Budila in the Anglo-Egyptian Sudan. The three flags are embroidered with the message 'Victory from Allah and a forthcoming conquest. Bring good news to the believers for God will give you a mighty victory'.
Photothèque, Musée de L'Homme. Catalog #64-12308-17

are his reward for carrying out a sacred religious obligation; for having fought against his oppressors by wielding the 'sword of truth' and for waging war 'in the way of God'.[5] This is surely an image of an all-encompassing religious ideology, a work that captures the fervour and passion of holy war in a way that recalls the words written by Sir Charles Wilson to describe the courage of one of the Mahdi's commanders killed in battle near the wells of Abu Tlaih:

> I saw a fine old Shaikh on horse back plant his banner in the center of the square, behind the camels. He was at once shot down falling on his banner. He turned out to be Musa, Amir of Dighaim Arabs, from Kurdufan. I had noticed him in the advance, with his banner in one hand and a book of prayers in the other, and never saw anything finer. The old man never swerved to the right or left, and never ceased chanting his prayers until he had planted his banner in our square. If any man deserved a place in the Moslem paradise he did.[6]

To fight with passion in 'the way of God' not only elevates a warrior's courage but it removes, in the event of earthly defeat, the sting of death and allows the martyr entry into Allah's paradise.

**33**

'God loves those who fight in His way . . .' Sura 61, verse 4. War horn used to signal and encourage the followers of the Mahdi in their wars against the British at the end of the nineteenth century.
Metropolitan Museum of Art. Michael C. Rockefeller Collection, purchase Nelson A. Rockefeller gift, 1965

33

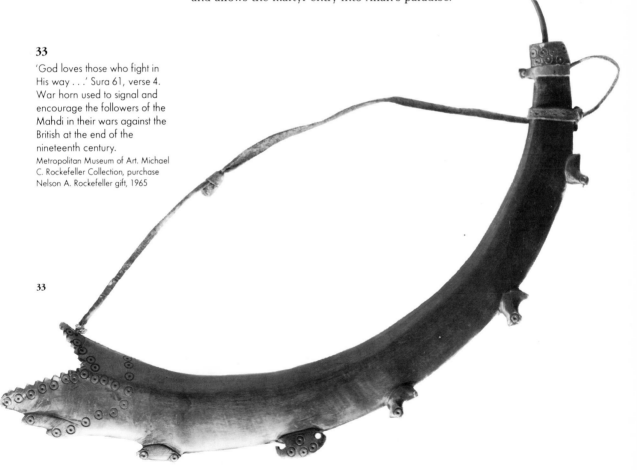

Musa the Dighaim Arab's courage and his closeness to God, described so well by Wilson, is what ultimately infuses this photograph with its potency. It tells us that Soliman Ziher confronted the military might of the British Empire with mere swords, ivory horns and embroidered flags and that most likely the majority of his followers were armed with nothing more than swords and sticks, a few clubs, their prayers and a belief in the holiness of their cause. The Mahdi's forces, of course, had captured sophisticated weapons, armour and chain-mail in their battles – indeed chain-mail, fine swords and battle axes were made in substantial numbers by the skilled metal craftsmen who accompanied the troops – but these do not form part of this carefully-composed image of victorious Islam. The broken and scattered remains of captured weapons are of little import in this montage for they are set apart and heaped unceremoniously upon the ground.

It is, rather, the presence of Allah and the passion of his followers for fighting in 'the way of God' that shine forth from this photograph. The three flags, embroidered with words and signs, evoke a sacred triptych, an altar erected in honour of man's duty to God. Each of the banners carries the same stentorian message – 'Victory from God and a forthcoming conquest. Bring good news to the believers for God will give you a mighty victory'.[7] They echo the words of Muhammad Ahmad, who wrote of a vision in which he received the crown of victory from the Prophet and was told 'There is no victory save from God . . . God has guarded you by His angels and prophets. No nation shall be able to face you in battle. . .'[8]

The message upon the flags is followed by seven signs:

$$6\ \wp\ \text{IIII}\ \#\ \text{T}\ \text{\#}\ \text{\AA}$$

that are together known as the seven seals or *khawatim* – mysterious marks said to represent the 'excellent names' or symbols of God. Only the first sign, the pentacle ⍟, appears to be understood: it is known as the seal of King Solomon and is believed to be derived from the design on a bezel on his ring. These powerful and magical shapes are further enhanced by numeric value, for the number 7 is particularly important in Islamic magic. Seven enumerates the fullness of Allah's creation, a reference to the dome of the seven heavens, the seven earths, seven seas, seven angels, the seven parts of the body used during prayer, the seven prophets and the seven hells with seven doors.[9] These flags, then, are indeed filled with God's presence and help us to appreciate the courage of men like Musa the Dighaim Arab who, in planting his banner within the square formed by the British troops at the battle of Abu Tlaih, welcomed death. In the same way, the flags of Soliman Ziher are imbued with special amuletic properties and express a sacred vision of holy war: carried high and in the forefront of battle they are like the banner of light seen hovering above the Mahdi's armies, a sign that he was indeed the Messiah and that his men were fighting in 'the way of God'.

In the Sudan the Mahdi's resistance movement, the Mahdiyya, had been active for nearly fifteen years when its leader died on 22 June 1895, nearly six months after Khartoum had fallen to the Mahdi's forces and General

Gordon had been killed. This crushing defeat had a profound effect upon Queen Victoria and her parliament and led to new and even more ferocious encounters between the British and the Mahdists. Abdullahi, Khalifa al-Mahdi, the Mahdi's successor, bore the full fury of British revenge and in decisive battles at Atbara and Omdurman (the latter literally in the shadows of destroyed Khartoum) Anglo-Egyptian forces under Kitchener routed the Khalifa's armies. By late November 1899 the Khalifa himself was mortally wounded at the battle of Om-Dubreikat, shattering the final hopes of a Mahdist state and making the Anglo-Egyptian Sudan a colonial reality.

It is in the nature of war that the victor establishes the full measure of his triumph, not only by counting the enemy dead but by bringing home evidence of his defeated foe, and the British forces in the Sudan proved no exception to this tradition. Those who have not been involved in battle seem to want and need the booty removed from the fallen victims nearly as much as do the warriors themselves. The more protracted and desperate the confrontation – and the Anglo-Egyptian campaigns against the Mahdi and his successor the Khalifa were surely both protracted and desperate – the greater the number of trophies collected as proof. With the flush of British victory in the Sudan the sheer quantity of war trophies brought back to England was impressive, a testament to the epic dimensions of the holy war waged by the Mahdists.

One of the most striking items brought home by the British was a large wooden slit drum, carved in the shape of a bullock, captured 'from the Khalifa' in the critical battle of Omdurman (Plate 34). There must be hundreds, possibly thousands, of items in European and American museums and in private collections that were captured from the defeated

**34**
Wooden slit drum captured from the Khalifa at the battle of Omdurman in the Anglo-Egyptian Sudan. The drum was presented to Queen Victoria by Lord Kitchener, commander of the Anglo-Egyptian forces.

**35**
An eighteenth-century Persian scimitar with the inscription 'There is no sword like Dhu'l faqar and no hero like Ali'.
Steel, brass and horn. 104 cm
Metropolitan Museum of Art, Rogers Fund 1977. #1977.162.7

**36**
This superb chain-mail hat with leather bound Koranic amulets was a particularly effective protective headgear. Acquired in the Anglo-Egyptian Sudan it was most likely made by armourers at Sennar, the capital of the Funj Kingdom south of Khartoum.
Iron, cotton, leather. 65.5 cm
UCLA, Museum of Cultural History, gift of the Wellcome Trust. #X65-8684

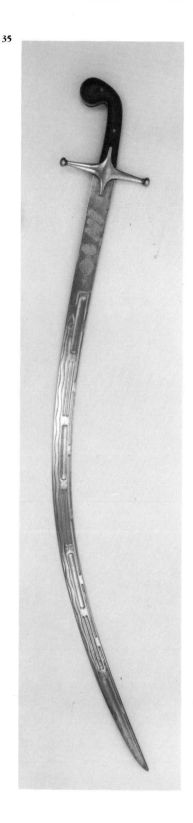

Mahdist troops, but few can compare with this monument. A massive sculpture, about 2.5m. in length, it was presented to Queen Victoria by Kitchener, who had been rewarded with a peerage for his role as commander at Omdurman and for ultimately crushing the Mahdist movement.[10] Lord Kitchener returned to England a hero of the Empire and his gift to the Queen, who had followed the events in the eastern Sudan so closely for nearly two decades, was a grand symbol of military victory.

There is more to this trophy than its scale, however, for it is a special kind of object, a drum that has long been associated with only the most prominent of chiefs and leaders in the southern Bahr-el-Ghazal region of the modern Republic of Sudan and in adjacent parts of the Central African Republic.[11] Drums such as these serve as voices of authority: they are the 'tongues of chiefs' and their size is dependent upon the rank of their royal owners. The enormous size of the Khalifa's drum testifies to his exalted status as the successor to the Mahdi and the booming sounds of this massively sculpted instrument must surely have encouraged his followers in battle.

Particularly intriguing are the incised designs along both sides of the bullock. Floral patterns and fret-like motifs are carved in a broad band across these surfaces, their geometric regularity reminiscent of the ancient Islamic shapes used to express God's unity and presence. A traditional African figurative drum form used in the service of the Khalifa and holy war has thus been emblazoned with patterns of Muslim belief.

Of the many objects captured in the wars fought against the Mahdists, or taken in the wake of various Islamic reform and resistance movements that swept Sudannic Africa from Senegal to the Red Sea in the eighteenth and nineteenth centuries, a substantial number demonstrate the desire to visualize certain aspects of God. Muslim armies invariably included clerics who not only fought bravely but whose prayers, Allah's words, elevated the spirits of the troops. Soldiers and cavalrymen covered themselves with robes, quilted clothing, chain-mail and headgear, and their horses with armour and trappings, all studded with amulets embracing God's words. Weaponry included bows and arrows, lances, shields, and later captured guns and cannons (or locally made copies of them), but it was the sword, straight-bladed or curved, that was the supreme Muslim fighting weapon and it too was often inscribed with Allah's name and his blessings. A particularly fascinating sword, reputedly captured at Omdurman and now in the arms and armour collection of the Metropolitan Museum of Art, demonstrates the desire for God's closeness in battle particularly well. (Plate 35) According to Helmut Nickel, curator of the collection, it is most likely an eighteenth-century Persian scimitar whose blade includes several grooves, a phrase inscribed in Arabic, and a snake etched in relief on each side of its outer or cutting edge. The most intriguing aspect of the sword has been described by Nickel:

> The blade is split lengthwise for about one quarter of its length, thus creating a blade with two points. This is in accordance with the apocryphal tradition that the sword of Muhammad – Dhu'l faqar – had two points or even two blades . . . That this double pointed scimitar is really meant to share in the glorious sword of the Prophet, which was once wielded in a decisive battle by the hero Ali [Muhammad's son-in-law and according to Shiite Muslims the legitimate successor to the Caliphate after the death of the Prophet], is indicated by its inscription: 'There is no sword like Dhu'l faqar and no hero like Ali'.[12]

A length of steel has thus been sanctified: like Ali, regarded by Shiites as the supreme warrior, saint and imam, its bearer would have wielded a finely honed 'sword of truth'.

That jihad was waged with the words and weapons of God is evident in many items associated with war. A superb chain-mail hat in the Museum of Cultural History at UCLA is generously adorned with leather-bound Koranic amulets and indicates again the need for Allah's words (Plate 36). The acquisition data simply indicate Sudan, but it is in fact a work from the Wellcome collection and may well have been collected by Wellcome himself in the Anglo-Egyptian Sudan where, just prior to the outbreak of the First World War, he directed an archaeological expedition near Khartoum.[13] It is reminiscent of Mameluke chain-mail workmanship of the fifteenth century, yet the form is a purely Sudannic innovation, for only in the Upper Nile region were hats fashioned of chain-mail. Des-

36

cendents of Mameluke armourers, however, may well have contributed technical expertise to the production of such pieces for many fled Egypt after its conquest by the Ottoman Turks and settled at Sennar, the capitol of the Funj kingdom that straddled the Blue Nile, some 320 km. up-river from Khartoum.[14] The owner of this fine head covering of chain-mail elevated his fighting spirit with the words of God, the surest protection for a soldier engaged in holy war.

A final example, also from the Wellcome Trust, is an unusual branched weapon with two halberd-like axe blades, an inspired attempt to impress the sounds of God upon yet another article of war (Plate 37). No documentation exists concerning its provenance, but the weapon may well have been fashioned in the southern stretches of either Wadai or Darfur, Muslim states in the Central Sudan, where throwing knives (very different in character but whose shapes are faintly echoed in this example) have been created by non-Muslim craftsmen for generations. Like traditional throwing knives, the weapon combines the shapely strength of iron with a wooden handle covered in leather and crocodile skin. What distinguishes the work, however, is its bulk and overtly aggressive char-acter: the fluid lines and elegant aerodynamic qualities of the throwing knife have been totally sacrificed in the search for an axe-like weapon that could be used in hand-to-hand combat. Particularly fascinating is the apparent desire of the artisan to temper this bellicose weapon by etching fine and shapely arabesques upon both sides of its iron branches. These shapes, neither Arabic conson-ants nor vowels, cannot be read, but they are unrelenting, completely covering the iron portions of the weapon. It would be easy enough to dismiss these signs as the unsuccessful attempt of an illiterate to emulate Arabic script, but this seems too simple an explanation, blinding one to the possibility of deeper intent. One feels, somehow, that these etched shapes have definite meaning even though they are not representative of any known language. In their ubiquity the incised designs seem to communicate the desire of the craftsman to capture the grace and flow of God's language and His inherent presence, and thus to enable both the weapon and its eventual owner to partake of Allah's words and being.

37

**37**

An aggressive looking branched iron weapon with wooden handle covered in crocodile skin and leather. The iron branches are filled with shapely arabesques in an attempt to emulate Arabic script.
Republic of Sudan or Chad? Iron, wood, leather, crocodile skin. 34 cm
UCLA, Museum of Cultural History, gift of the Wellcome Trust.
#X-67-561

**38**

Chain-mail shirts were worn by Fulani and Kanuri cavalrymen — flexible armour was ideally suited to such warriors. This example, and indeed much of the chain-mail used in Northern Nigeria, is of sixteenth and seventeenth century Mameluke manufacture.
Kanuri, Nigeria. Chain links wedge riveted. 86.5 cm
Royal Ontario Museum. #961-141-50
Gift of Dr. Ronald Cohen

**39**

This Nupe saddle with cotton embroidery is one of the many items of booty taken from the defeated Fulani forces at the turn of the century. Nupe formed part of the Fulani Empire and this emirate fought nobly against the British colonial forces.

Nupe, Nigeria. Leather, cotton. 68.5 cm
Department of Anthropology, American Museum of Natural History, 68.5 cm

**40**

A cotton war belt from Mangu, northern Togo, with the inscription 'In the Name of God the Compassionate'. Allah was constantly invoked and his praises chanted, by the soldiers of the faith.

Mangu, Togo. Cotton, coloured inks. 110 cm
Field Museum of Natural History. #104.803

**41**

A Jibbeh, or tunic, worn by an officer of the Mahdi's army dating from the period 1885–1899. Wool-felt appliqué and embroidered chainstitch designs.

Republic of Sudan. Cotton, wool. 136 cm
Lowie Museum of Anthropology. (University of California, Berkeley) #48.29.62

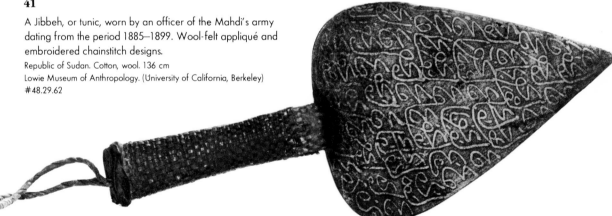

**42**

An unusual heart-shaped iron knife with a wooden handle wrapped with leather. Arabesque entirely covers both sides of the blade in a passionate demonstration of ennobling an object with the words of God.

Republic of Sudan. Wood, iron, leather. 48 cm
UCLA, Museum of Cultural History, gift of the Wellcome Trust. #65-1998

# CHAPTER FOUR

# Ramadan – Islamic holy days and an African sensibility

To witness thousands of believers moving together in prayer at the conclusion of the month-long fast of Ramadan is unforgettable. The festival, known as *Id al Fitr*, is conducted in Bobo-Dioulasso in Upper Volta in a large open space just to the east of the Rue de l'Imam Sakidi Sanou and approximately 400 metres from the oldest mosque in the city by the Place du President Ouezzin Coulibaly. *Id al Fitr* occurs on the first day of *Shawwal*, the month following Ramadan, and is regarded primarily as a day of feasting and relaxation after the rigours of the fast. For the faithful the day begins with a public prayer and an enthralling display of religious solidarity and community. Men, women and children, dressed in their finest clothing, come from all points within the city to this laterite plaza, arriving by mid-morning to spread their prayer mats on the ground. The men arrange themselves according to age and their residence within the city and sit towards the front, closest to the imam and other religious notables; the women and children find the best available places behind the men. What is most striking about this vast community of believers, however, is its uniformity. It is a crowd clad almost entirely in white: men wear long white gowns and skull caps, some of which are embroidered in white or light pastel colours; women dress in white blouses and skirts or waist cloths; and children are clothed in the style and colour of their parents, looking very much like miniature versions of them.

Despite the importance of *Id al Fitr* it is a surprisingly short religious service consisting of two *rak'as*, or bowings, that accompany the reciting of the prayers, and a two-part *Khutba*, or formal homily, delivered by the imam. The entire service lasts barely an hour; what impresses the observer is the vast sea of white that sways, bends from side to side, and gracefully prostrates itself accompanying the muffled sounds of chanting and prayer. All the believers face east towards Mecca with a common purpose, a shared heart and mind, and their unity is overwhelming: they have gathered to worship on this morning, as have Muslims throughout the world, in order to proclaim in unison the majesty and goodness of Allah and to thank him for having brought them through the trying month-long fast.

Yet this apparent unity and solidarity is something of an illusion, for while Islam is fully capable of minimizing and indeed submerging the many differences among its adherents, especially at moments like *Id al Fitr*, such an assemblage of people is ultimately diverse and separates itself into its constituent parts at the conclusion of the service. Among the several thousand worshippers are Dyula, Zara and recently converted Bobo whose families have lived in Bobo-Dioulasso for generations. There are also Muslims from as far away as Senegal and Nigeria, the Wolof and Hausa for example, who have settled within the city only recently. The variety of faces and cultures among these believers must be recognized and fully appreciated.

It is precisely this element of diversity, of cultural strength and creativity within the larger community of African Islam, that I want to explore. I shall attempt this by looking at the month-long ritual of Ramadan and how it is observed among the Dyula of Upper Volta and Ivory

44

Shape is a
Roman
tabula ansata
(tablet with a handle)

[ansa, ae = handle]

Coast.[1] Muslim festivals like Ramadan are a particularly apt example of the remarkable diversity of practice found within African Islam, for they are among the most basic institutional forms of the faith, yet wholly subject to the religious and expressive needs of its believers. African Islamic festivals are vivid enactments of religious sentiments, public demonstrations of communal commitment, and because they are often elaborate, unfolding over time, they have a rhythm and life of their own that can be examined and thought about. To look at such festivals is to confront the full force of culture and artistry as they shape and focus religious doctrine and belief itself. Examining the Dyula observance of Ramadan should enable us to see how one Muslim culture has come to practice the obligatory period of the fast by merging a religious ideal with ancient Dyula values and sensibilities.

The great fast of Ramadan, surely the most arduous of all Islamic rituals, takes its name from the ninth month of the Muslim calendar year. Among the Dyula the period is appropriately called *Sunkalo*, the moon of deprivation, and it is said that not only is the month-long fast trying but that life itself is turned upon its head. Night becomes day, for it is only between sunset and sunrise that one may eat, drink, engage in gossip, or enjoy sexual intercourse. The daylight hours are reserved for reflection and self-examination; they are dedicated to Allah through the abstention from all earthly desires. Fasting is crucial, being one of the five pillars of the faith, and its importance to Muslims everywhere has perhaps been expressed best (according to von Grunebaum) by the great eleventh-century theologian and legal thinker Ghazzali:

> it represents one quarter of faith, for the Prophet said: fasting is one half of endurance, and he also said: endurance is one half of faith. And the Prophet is also credited with the observation that the foul smell of the faster's mouth is sweeter before God than the scent of musk.[2]

Ghazzali elaborated upon the special merits of fasting. Contemplation of the Divine, he said, can only occur when there 'is no barrier of food between chest and heart', fasting, 'unlike all other devotional acts, is visible only to God', and for the faithful fasting is 'the gateway of divine service'.[3] The Dyula would surely agree with all these words, for they describe fasting as an act that enlarges the believer's voice so that he may be heard by Allah.

The rigours of the fast are readily visible in any African Muslim community, and especially among the Dyula who conspicuously follow its proscriptions. Dyula towns and villages, normally distinguished by their intense commercial activity and personal vivacity, are remarkably muted places during the daylight hours of Ramadan. Attendance at mosques increases dramatically and the pious spend these days reading large portions of the Koran, some completing the entire work within the month, others capable of two or three complete readings during this period. Ramadan is regarded as a time for religious instruction and people congregate to listen to the words of teachers and elders who expound upon the meaning of the fast and its obligations.

**45**

This cotton and wool appliqué gown is known as a Rabih gown. Rabih ibn Fad'l Allah, who ruled Bornu from 1893–1899, created the trappings of a Mahdist state whose influence extended even to modes of dress. This gown, related both in style and technique to the Mahdi Jibbeh or tunic, is still worn by Muslim notables at major Islamic festivals.

Kanuri, Nigeria. Cotton, wool. 168 cm
Field Museum of Natural History.
#221.522

Fasting, according to the Dyula, is essential, for it purifies the believers' minds and hearts, allowing greater access to Allah's words and blessings. To observe the fast faithfully is particularly important, for to follow God's directives during this month is said to be thirty times more beneficial than at other times during the calendar year. Most Dyula clearly take to heart the Koranic injunction: 'complete the Fast unto the night . . . cleave to the mosques. Those are God's bounds; keep well within them'.[4]

That life is inverted, that the nights of Ramadan bring a release from the demands of the day, is obvious in any Dyula setting. In this respect the Dyula also follow those words of the Koran that serve as a guide for night-time behaviour during the fast: 'eat and drink, until the white thread shows clearly to you from the black thread at dawn.'[5] While there is time for prayer during these nights, they are also meant for socializing and feasting and throughout the Muslim world they are marked by various forms of entertainment. Among the Dyula these nights (and those of the succeeding month of *Shawwal*) are highlighted by an unusual degree of creativity.

45

## 46

Wooden mask of a feline head that is wrapped in hide and has glass eyes. The painted patterns are highly reminiscent of wall paintings from Walata in Mauretania and have strong Islamic associations. The context for this mask is not known.
Bozo (?), Republic of Mali. Wood, paint, hide, glass. 52 cm
The D. and J. de Menil Collection, Houston

## 47

*Siginkura-ayna*, and other *do* masks, perform the entire first week after the month of Ramadan in Ligbi villages. This festival, known as *mingare tulu* 'the feast of the Moon of drinking and pleasure', is a time of levity and goodness during which the Ligbi perform these dances of joy and beauty.
Ligbi, Ivory Coast. Wood, paint. 31 cm
Seattle Art Museum. Katherine White Collection. #81.17 264

## 48

Do masks are oiled, repainted and often given items of jewellery for their performances after Ramadan. They are, in fact, very much like their human counterparts for, *mingare tulu* is a time when people wear new clothes, beautify themselves, and revel in the passing of the fast.
Ligbi, Ivory Coast. Wood, pigments. 34 cm
National Museum of African Art, Smithsonian Institution. Bequest of Samuel Rubin. #79.61.21

**49**

A dignified and turbaned Muslim northerner, most likely a representation of a Hausa man, is portrayed in this *gelede* mask honouring the ever-increasing influence of Islam in Yoruba life.
Yoruba, Nigeria. Wood, pigment. 43 cm
Valerie Franklin Collection

**50**

*Simma* is a masquerade performed by farmers in the highly stratified and heavily Islamized states of Gonja and Wa in northern Ghana. Such masks reveal the levels of coexistence possible between Islam and traditional religions and creativity.
Vagala, N.W. Ghana. Wood, iron, and pigment. 44 cm.
Lent by UCLA, Museum of Cultural History. #LX80-226

**51**

A fine example of a 3-dimensional child's *dodo* mask.
Mossi, from the capital city of Ouagadougou, Upper Volta. Gourd,
paint, stalks, wire and string. 31 cm
Seattle Art Museum (Katherine White Collection) #81.17.113

**52**

Members of a *dodo* troupe who have prepared
themselves for their Ramadan performance. Photograph
taken in Bobo Dioulasso, Upper Volta.
Author's photograph, October 1972

On any given evening in Bobo-Dioulasso Dyula children between the ages of six and fifteen perform *dodo*, a masquerade to entertain the community and reward those who perform it. *Dodo* is an enchanting phenomenon, wholly orchestrated and directed by children, who make masks, work out choreographic and acrobatic routines for each masked character, and create songs sung by the chorus that accompanies each *dodo* troupe. *Dodo* celebrates the artistry and ingenuity of childhood for it is created from tattered pieces of cloth, scraps of cardboard, fractured and discarded gourds, humble earth pigments, and the occasional small vial of imported paint, all artfully combined with youthful imagination. A *dodo* troupe consists of close friends who plan which masked characters will be produced, who will dance them, and who will serve as musicians. Masks of animals are particularly popular and generally include the lion (*wara*), the ugly wild pig (*kongo-liu*), the greedy monkey (*soula*) and a large and very pregnant bull elephant (*sama*). A *dodo* masked performance may also portray the miserly elder or a popular culture personality like the reggae musician Bob Marley. Each *dodo* troupe is led by one of the oldest boys who brandishes a stick to protect the ensemble from potential danger. He wears *yogoro*, a mask made out of cardboard with two horns of millet stalks.

These masks are made just before the onset of Ramadan and *dodo* members work together, the older and more experienced boys tutoring and helping those who are younger and less adept. Sections of old gourds are generally used as a base, for their natural shapes conform nicely to the face and require only minimal cutting and working to serve as masks: an old knife for trimming, a hot poker for boring the holes for eyes, nose and mouth, and a large needle for sewing tight any cracks in the gourds are the only tools necessary. Sticks that have been chewed at one end to form rudimentary brushes and one's fingers are all that are needed to apply paint and the black, tar-like substance used to highlight the features of the masks. Horns, trunks, ears and other attachments are made from a variety of found materials and lashed to the gourds with strips of cloth, string, or locally-made cord. Masks that fit more fully over the head (as in the example from the Katherine White Collection of the Seattle Art Museum), are made of several gourd sections stitched together and secured at various points (Plate 51). Every afternoon during Ramadan the members of the *dodo* group paint the dancers' bodies with natural white clay, *bugogwe*, mixed with water and used to create patterns that befit each masked character.

*Dodo* groups circulate throughout the Dyula quarter of Kongbougou nightly, moving from house to house and playing in courtyards if they are invited in. Each masked dancer has his turn – his drum rhythm is tapped out by the small musicians on old tin cans and he is encouraged by a chorus of boys, and sometimes girls, who sing the appropriate songs. One of the most popular characters is *soula*, the greedy and capricious monkey who goes about with an open paw demanding food, money, cloth, indeed whatever his imaginative mind and greed suggest at any given moment. *Dodo* is sheer entertainment and those who perform with skill and charm are rewarded because, as the children realize only too well, the nights of Ramadan are meant to be joyous and they are times when people tend to demonstrate their generosity.[6]

The night before the 15th of Ramadan is an important celebration among the Dyula. It is called *Kurubi-deni* or *Kurubi Fitini* – 'the small night when one does not sleep'. Falling on one of the 'white nights', when the moon is full, *Kurubi-deni* always

provides a splendid display of beauty and solidarity and ushers in a day which is considered by many to be particularly important and auspicious for fasting. On this night many of the faithful gather to hear readings from the Koran and to learn about the special merits of the fast; it is also a time when young men drum and dance, but they do so separately from the women, who are the real focus of attention. I have observed *Kuribi-deni* on two different occasions in Bobo-Dioulasso, in October 1972 and June 1982. Both performances were similar to what Quimby observed among the same Dyula in 1969 and to Marcel Prouteaux's description of *Courvi-Fitini* among the Dyula of Kong, some 400 kilometres to the south in Ivory Coast nearly fifty years earlier.[7] The parallels to the *Courvi-Fitini* performance are striking and seem to confirm the intimate historical connections between the Dyula of these two communities, for the Dyula of Bobo-Dioulasso invariably trace their origins back to nineteenth-century Kong.

*Kurubi-deni* begins late in the evening, well after everyone has relaxed and the men have returned from services at the mosque. It is performed until dawn. The broad features of the performance have been noted already by Quimby:

> 'One group of dancers comprised the unmarried girls. They wore only rather scanty briefs made of cotton, their hair was elaborately coiffed, their bodies were decorated with splashes of white flour-and-water paste, and they wore the largest and most ornate gold necklaces their families could afford. They carried a horse tail in each hand, to wave as they danced . . . They danced in a circle, clapping and singing to the accompaniment of a drummer. Their songs were frequently satirical and composed on the spur of the moment. Some of the dancers carried rattles. The women who had been married 5 years or more danced with the girls, but dressed in pagnes and without the special hairdressing. Older women often stood at the side, clapping and singing. Each lineage held its own dances.[8]

The dances at the *Kuribi-deni* in 1982 were marked by their stylized beauty and elegance. Each of the groups danced in a large circle or in file and the young girls' movements, carried out with stunning unity, consisted of short, almost imperceptible steps and a graceful ripple of the upper body that began in the shoulders and flowed through the entire length of the arms. The atmosphere was one of leisure and it was captured in the body and self-possession of each performer.

On this particular evening the young girls wore waistcloths, as they did in Kong in the early 1920s, and several of the young female dancers carried plain wooden canes. Prouteaux mentioned such canes, but those he described were elaborately decorated with alternating bands of animal hide and red and green cotton cloth, and had strands of cowries and small brass bells suspended at intervals along their length. Young men, according to lineages, also perform strong and vigorous dances in Bobo-Dioulasso but apparently they did not do so in Kong.[9] Details aside, *Kuribi-deni* has been performed by the Dyula with considerable consistency since the early part of this century and it continues to highlight the middle of the month-long fast. Carried out by young women and men who display their youth and beauty, it is an assertion that the Dyula follow God's proscriptions during this month and retain their strength despite its rigours.

An even more elaborate celebration occurs on the night prior to the 27th of Ramadan, the *Kurubi-Ba* or great night when one does not sleep, and then during the daytime on the remaining days of the month. *Kurubi-Ba* is a tribute to God for it is on this night, known as *Lailat al-Kadr* or the 'Night of Power', that Allah first revealed the Koran to Muhammad. The special character and magic of this night is explicitly stated in Sura 97 of the Koran, the chapter known as *al Kadr.*

> Behold, we sent it down on the Night of Power;
> And what shall teach thee what is
> the Night of Power?
> The Night of Power is better than a
> thousand months;
> in it the angels and Spirit descend,
> by the leave of their Lord, upon every command.
> Peace it is, till the rising of dawn.[10]

Among the Dyula this is a night of special grace, for the evil spirits or *jinn*, who have been chained by God's angels since the onset of Ramadan, are now doubly and triply bound and the gates of heaven are opened allowing the good angels and the spirit of God to descend into the world. On this night,

Koranic students take the opportunity to visit the graves of the family dead to deliver Allah's blessings to the ancestors. The knowledge of his presence is not only reassuring, it brings out that special Dyula sensibility for parading joy and closeness to God.[11]

*Kurubi-Ba*, as the name implies, is an enlarged version of *Kurubi-deni* held twelve days earlier, and an artistic display that honours the revelatory nature of *Lailat al-Kadr*. The numbers of dancers and drummers from each Dyula lineage are now much larger and there is a sense of aesthetic competition that does not exist at *Kurubi-deni*. Each group of unmarried girls is led by a single dancer, clad only in briefs and strands of colourful waist beads, her entire body covered with beautifully patterned designs made from a rice flour and water paint (Plate 53). The designs are carefully rendered and consist of elegant lines, squares and rectangles, circles and a variety of grid patterns. Appropriate shifts in pattern occur at various points of the body and are accomplished with such skill that each part receives due attention, yet does not detract from an appreciation of the overall unity of body design. Each of the dance leaders carries on her head a set of from six to eight stacked brass or imported enamel basins containing medicines and cowries tied in a large string net. A necklace with leather amulets attached, a colourful headtie that completely covers the hair and a narrow piece of cloth tied around the torso complete the attire.

53

By the light of kerosene lamps and small candles carried by young children, these strikingly-painted figures move slowly through Kongbougou followed by girls and musicians of their own lineages. They stop at the houses of respected elders and relatives to dance and sing and then move on to perform in adjacent neighbourhoods and at the large market in the heart of the city. The dancing and singing are reminiscent of *Kurubi-deni*, but there is a greater intensity and character which can be felt in the

54

shared and heightened intimacy between drummers, chorus and dancers. Dressed in white waistcloths, with gold and silver jewellery upon their bodies and in their hair the girls form a sparkling ensemble in the available lamplight. Two pressure drums, their pitches varied with dazzling speed, and a solo calabash drum with ringed metal flanges adding a metallic shimmer to its driving sound, encourage the voices and bodies by praising their beauty and elegance. The dancers in turn heap praises upon the drummers, enabling each to share in the other's glory. The drumming and dancing continue until dawn when the call to prayer is heard throughout every Dyula community. Minor festive displays resume in the afternoon and for the next two to three days as people anxiously await the new moon of Shawwal. When the new moon has been sighted the Dyula prepare themselves for *Id al Fitr*, the public prayer that occurs in the morning, and for the days of joy and feasting that follow the end of Ramadan.

In Bobo-Dioulasso, life during the first two weeks of Shawwal is described as God's gift to his believers, and is marked by dances, opulent meals and people revelling in each other's company. It is a time when one wears new clothing and parades with one's friends. For some it is also a period when normal precautions must be taken – a time to incense one's house so that it will be protected from the *jinn* unleashed by the end of the fast. Life has been turned right side up once again and there is a gradual return to everyday concerns.

In certain Dyula communities the period following *Id al Fitr* may include other forms of artistry interspersed with the formal sounds of prayer and feasting. Among the Dyula of Bondoukou, in the eastern Ivory Coast, until recently masked dancers performed every night for an entire week after Ramadan. This was noted by several French observers early in this century and apparently continued until the mid-1950s when the masks were finally abandoned because such dances were considered inappropriate to breaking the fast.[12] In the late 1960s, however, many Dyula families from Bondoukou still attended such masquerades, known as *do*, performed in the nearby villages of Ligbi and Hwela, two Muslim peoples closely related to the Dyula.[13]

At Kong, Prouteaux recorded that on the afternoon of *Id al Fitr* and for eight days thereafter, the town was full of excitement and people expressed their joy through dance at the passing of the fast. He also noted that a multi-coloured banner, crowned with two carved birds, was paraded at a dance called *sabe* just before sunset on the day of the *Id*.[14] Beginning on the 8th or 9th of Shawwal the Dyula were further regaled by a variety of masquerades that performed for an entire week: colourful cloth-masked characters known as *Kondali* and *Toro* (or *Tro*) who acted as buffoons and delighted their audience; carefully carved wooden masks, some covered with brass, known as *lo* that were elegantly decorated with jewellery in the manner of the young girls who danced at the Kurubi ceremonies (Plate 54). At the very end of the week appeared the *safo*, a lone masquerader wearing a jet black hood vertically bisected by a strong red band of cloth whose body was fully enveloped in fibres.[15] These traditions continue in Kong today, serving as a conclusion to Ramadan and a testament to the aesthetic sensibilities of the Muslim Dyula.[16]

# CHAPTER FIVE

---

# al-Burāq –
# African variations upon an
# Ancient Islamic theme

At the great market in the city of Kumase, ancient capital of the Asante 56
people of Ghana, one can find truly anything. On almost any day it is filled
with people buying and selling the most humble and exotic items, and it
was among a group of Muslim booksellers, at the extreme edge of this vast
bazaar, that I first encountered the image of al-Burāq. I was browsing
through books and manuscripts when I noticed a print of a curious white
winged creature: it had the body of a horse but its head was that of a
beautiful woman, with long dark hair, wearing a heavily jewelled and
plumed crown. This riderless steed had elegant peacock feathers for a tail,
mighty wings upon its back and a colourful saddle blanket with Arabic
script embroidered upon it. It wore anklets on its four legs, just above the
hooves. I was told by the elderly bookseller that this was a picture of al-
Burāq, Muhammad's winged horse, and that the artist had depicted her in
flight just as it is written in the Koran. He told me that he sold many such
prints and that he obtained them from a relative who was living in Niamey
in Niger, but that they all came from Egypt. I have since learned that my
print, for I could not resist it, can be obtained from Hussain's Bookstore
and Printing Press at 18 Mashad Al Hussaini, in Cairo. The artist was Abd'
al-Hamid Ahmad Hanafi.

Since my discovery of this image of al-Burāq I have seen many more,
some for sale in other West African markets and shops, others in the
homes of Muslims and non-Muslims where they are framed and conspicuously placed on a sitting-room wall or in more private quarters.
Printing houses in Egypt, Algeria and Tunisia have spawned something of
a minor tradition of images like the one of al-Burāq and other religious
subjects, which are mass-produced, inexpensive and wonderfully literal,
highly accessible depictions. Of all the subjects treated (those most often
seen include Muhammad's heroic battle at Badr, pilgrims on the hadj, a
saint's tomb and a generalized rendering of the Mosque of the Dome of the
Rock in Jerusalem), surely the most popular is the one of al-Burāq.

A particularly fine example of al-Burāq is a version, most likely printed
in Algeria, in the Lowie Museum of Anthropology that was collected in the
late 1940s somewhere in Ghana.[1] The principal colours of this print are
deep reds and plum which are particularly rich, but the work is also more
finely detailed than most recent examples and is more generously
endowed with religious inscriptions (Plate 56). Within the broad border
surrounding the print, and between the various medallions, is the first
verse of Sura 17 of the Koran, known as 'The Israelite' or 'The Night
Journey':

> In the name of Allah, the Beneficent, the Merciful
> Praised be He who carried his servant
> at night from the sacred Mosque to the Distant Mosque,
> whose precincts we blessed that we might show Him our signs.
> Indeed, He is the Hearing, the Seeing.
> Allah, the Mighty, speaks the Truth.[2]

The medallions in the upper left- and right-hand corners carry the names
'Muhammad' and 'Allah' and the rectangular box just above the wings of al-

Modèle Déposé, E.B.

**55 (title page)**
Baga drum from Guinea with
caryatid figure of al-Burāq.
Baga, Guinea. 170 cm
Royal Ontario Museum

**56**

This print of Muhammad's winged steed al-Burāq was collected in Ghana in the late 1940s. Within the border surrounding the print is the first verse of Sura 17 of the Koran known as the Night Journey. In the rectangular box above the wings of al-Burāq is the praise 'al-Buraq, the Noble and Sympathetic friend'.

Algeria or Tunisia, paper and inks. 45 cm     Lowie Museum of Anthropology (Berkeley) #5-10184

Burāq is filled with the phrase 'al-Burāq, the noble and sympathetic friend'. Around the saddle blanket al-Burāq is extolled once again – 'Praised be he who carried his servant (to) the distant mosque'.[3]

That the image of al-Burāq has found a most comfortable home in Africa is not only visible in these popular prints but in Islamic verse (both in Arabic and in local languages written in Arabic script). It is revealed too through a range of artistry that surely commands our attention.[4] To my mind the popularity of al-Burāq is based upon the powers associated with this winged steed, which is said to have carried the Prophet on his mystical night journey (*Isra*) from Mecca to Jerusalem and then on his nocturnal ascent (*al-Miraj*) to the dome of the seven heavens. The owners of these prints describe the subject matter in tones bordering upon awe for it comprehends a series of events redolent with mystery and immanence. Muslims in Africa and elsewhere regard al-Burāq as the vehicle that made possible both the night journey and ascension, two crucial occurences in the life of Muhammad told of in part by Koranic revelation and then developed in religious commentaries and elaborated by the artistic and popular imagination. The name and images of al-Burāq allow the believer entry into the fullness and mystery of Islamic cosmology, its celestial bodies, religious symbols, angels and malign spirits, and ultimately the throne of God. Al-Burāq is a vital part of this religious epic, a part replete with miracles that both instruct and enchant, and enable the believer to contemplate the kingdom of heaven and the presence of Allah.

The clearest Koranic reference to this dramatic theme is the short verse from Sura 17 noted around the border of the Lowie Museum print. Others such as #40 v.38, #28 v.3 and #52 v.38 suggest the possibility of an ascension but they are far too cryptic and essentially unconnected fragments of religious revelation.[5] The words shimmer with mystical import but are so elliptical and undeveloped that one can barely recognize them for their epic potential. The elaboration of these barest intimations into a tale of cosmic proportions begins to emerge only in the centuries following the Koran with the writings of the Koranic commentators, in the Hadith literature of Tabari, Bukhari, Muslim and Ibn Abbas and others, who firmly bring together and embroider with detail the Prophet's nocturnal journey and his ascension astride al-Burāq.

It is in the Hadiths that we begin to witness the episodes of a true legend: the appearance of the heavenly messenger Gabriel before Muhammad at Mecca; the washing and purification of the Prophet's heart (an act that prepares him for the ascent and his initiation into the highest of mysteries and knowledge); the Prophet's voyage from Mecca to Jerusalem and his flight through the sky and its celestial gates upon al-Burāq. Muhammad's journey into the seven heavenly spheres, accompanied by Gabriel, and his visits to paradise and to the wretched sinners relegated to hell; his discussions with earlier messengers of God, the prophets of the Old and New Testament; and finally the eschatological vision of Muhammad meeting with the creator, where he comes before God himself, are also delineated. The commentaries specifically develop the image of al-Burāq for it is variously described as a donkey-like creature or as a noble horse with wings upon its shanks that enable it to move with the speed of lightning.[6]

**57**
This small al-Burāq sculpture
was collected by William
Bascom in Ghana in the 1940s,
although it is doubtful whether it
is of African workmanship.
Indian or Ghanaian?
Lowie Museum of Anthropology,
University of California (Berkeley)

While the canonical writers of Hadith were to establish a secure place
for this theme within the religious literature of Islam, its fullest flowering
came with future generations of poets and painters. Poetry and painting,
either alone or when used to enrich each other as in the many jewel-like
manuscripts devoted to the Prophet's life, convey even more deeply and
magically these marvellous events. Biographies (*sira*) of the Prophet, based
not only upon the known facts surrounding his life but also incorporating
the many miracles attributed to him, were extremely popular and they
invariably contained rather lengthy and highly dramatic expositions of the
crucial scenes of the ascension. Islamic praise poetry, known as *Madih*,
also flourished and proved a particularly apt medium for the legend's
formal patterning. The poetry's dense and rhythmic repetition of ideas and
imagery serve as a perfect vehicle for this emotionally charged theme.

In no area of Islamic literature, however, was the influence of the night
journey, the ascension and al-Burāq itself felt more profoundly than
among Sufi authors who took the legend as a virtual metaphor for their
own existence. Muhammad's transcendent voyage was the passage that all
Sufi sought to emulate, a path that all mystics attempted to follow in their
own lives.[7] The ascension became the single most important theme in Sufi
mysticism, shaped and reshaped as a tale of ultimate aspiration. For Sufi
writers, al-Burāq emerged as 'the noble and sympathetic friend', the

heavenly creature that conveys the believer with grace and swiftness to the divine proximity. In Sufi allegories, as de Treville suggests, al-Burāq becomes the vehicle 'by which abnegation is made possible and earthly attachments may be severed in reaching God'.[8]

In fifteenth- and sixteenth-century Persia, Sufi poets and painters, who were not necessarily themselves Sufists, conspired to produce some of the most remarkable illustrated manuscripts of Muhammad's life, and specifically of his ascension upon the winged al-Burāq. Ascension miniatures of this period are masterpieces of concentrated artistry, riveting the viewer's attention to the detailed miracle of the Prophet's journey across a luminous sky. Despite their small size, these are grandly conceived paintings combining rich colours and movement in such an intoxicating manner that the eye and mind, held in thrall, become transported as if the viewer were upon the wing of mystical fervour. All are dominated by a deep blue sky filled with clouds, angels and celestial activity, but at the heart of these jewel-like paintings, at their still centres, the Prophet sits majestically upon the crowned and human-headed al-Burāq. These glimpses of the cosmos and of Muhammad's transcendent flight are not only beautiful to behold but they are, as T.W. Arnold has suggested, revelations of Muhammad as the chosen Prophet:

> There was no event in the Prophet's life that had so triumphantly indicated his claim to be the 'Apostle of God and the seal of the Prophets' (Qur'an, xxxiii. 40) . . . his ascension had raised him to a level such as no ordinary mortal had attained; he had gazed upon the face of God Himself . . .[9]

Such images indelibly confirmed Muhammad's prophethood and testified to the power of his celestial mount.

Sixteenth-century Persian miniatures of the ascension honour al-Burāq with the head of a beautiful woman wearing a discreetly proportioned crown. Her equine body is elegantly shaped with a long, graceful back and sweeping tail. She is full-bodied and achieves her stride with slender yet powerful legs. Al-Burāq is generally white, sometimes dappled, with small wings on her shanks. When Persian painting declined in the seventeenth century, depictions of this noble theme, and particularly the treatment of al-Burāq, deteriorated markedly. According to Arnold, the new and vulgarized versions of al-Burāq that began to appear have persisted to the present:

> her appearance was certainly not improved by the addition of an ill-shaped, heavy crown, such as that worn by later Shahs of Persia, or by the substitution of an upstanding peacock's tail . . . Even to the present day, crude pictures of Burāq, without her rider, are popular in Egyptian villages and flimsy representations of this strange beast are carried in Muharram processions in India.[10]

Yet it is these 'crude pictures', which seem such a source of embarrassment to Arnold, that are so popular in Africa and that may in part have served as visual catalysts for the wonderfully creative renditions of al-Burāq currently being produced by African sculptors and scribes.

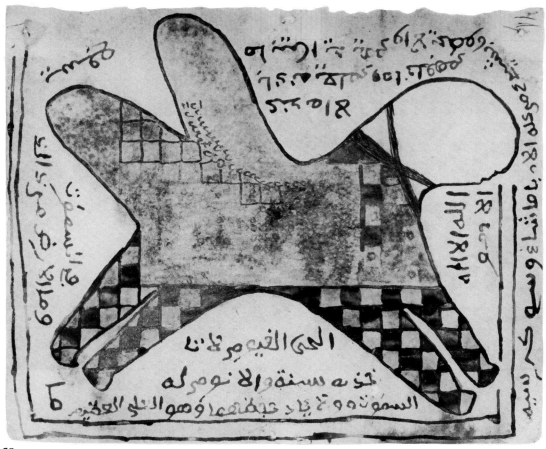

**58**

A hatumere, or amulet, of the winged al-Burāq surrounded
by portions of the second Sura, verse 235, the *Ayat al-Kursi*,
describing the power and immanence of Allah.

Fulbe/Limba, Sierra Leone. Paper and coloured inks. 21.5 cm
Collection of Simon Ottenberg

A particularly fascinating example, one that
captures the immanent quality of the ascension
and the essence of al-Burāq, is a small amulet
collected by Ottenberg at Bafodea in northern
Sierra Leone (Plate 58). The charm, written and
drawn in black, orange, purple and sepia inks on
graph paper, is referred to locally as *amburaku* (al-
Burāq). It is dominated by a highly stylized and
riderless figure of al-Burāq in flight, surrounded on
all sides by portions of Koranic verse, known as the
Hatal-Krusu at Bafodea. The verse is actually
number 235 of the second Sura, the *Ayat al-Kursi* or
'Throne Verse', the glorious passage that describes
Allah's throne (before which Muhammad was
transported by al-Burāq) embracing the heavens,
the earth and indeed the entire fabric of his
creation.[11] In this amulet a riderless al-Burāq,
having travelled through a measureless expanse to
reach the throne of God, is surrounded by the
divine proximity.

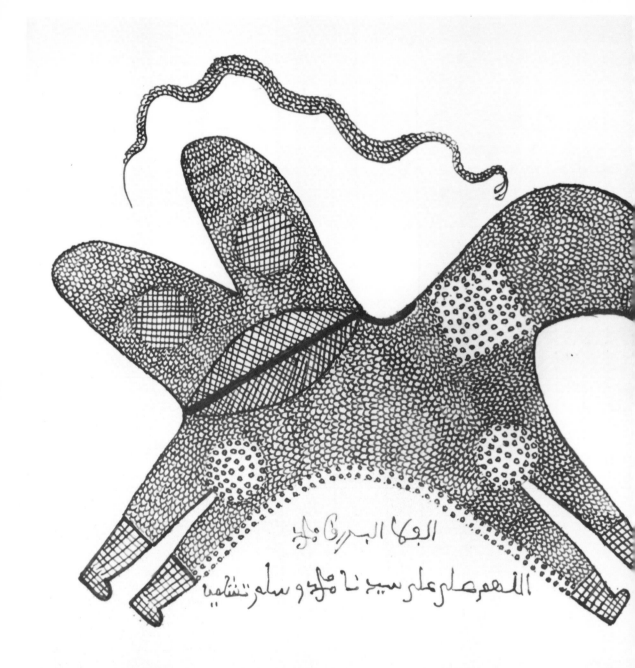

**59**   Another hatumere of al-Burāq (*Amburaku*) clearly related to the amulet of al-Burāq shown in Plate 58. This hatumere also includes the throne verse, called *Hatal Krusu* (*Ayat al-Kursi*) but here it is neatly written within a framed border and includes an 'angel snake' drawn above the winged al-Burāq.

Limba, Sierra Leone. Paper and black ink. 33 cm
Collection of Simon Ottenberg.

The Limba of Bafodea regard *amburaku* as a very powerful charm particularly effective as a deterrent to *tasalima* or witches. An *amburaku* is generally left unfolded and placed above a doorway to guard against the entry of witches: a powerful sentinel, it is said to be capable of killing witches within a matter of days.[12] Its protective capabilities are twofold, stemming from the written verse and the drawing. The words surrounding the amulet proclaim the fullness of Allah's power and majesty and thereby assert that the home in which it is found is under his protective gaze: the winged al-Burāq, that moves like the flash of lightning according to legend, will deflect all witches who use their ability to fly in order to wreak havoc and kill.

In Freetown, the coastal capital of Sierra Leone, masked manifestations of an elegant al-Burāq are carried in a public display known as 'Lanterns', a wonderful contrast to amuletic depictions of the winged steed. Performed at the end of Ramadan on *Id al Fitr*, 'Lanterns' celebrates the end of the fast and the vitality of urban life with stunning artistry. The spectacle, according to John Nunley, was first noted by Robert Wellesley Cole in his reminiscences of childhood, *Kossoh Town Boy*.[13] Born at the turn of the century into a staunch Christian Krio family, Cole grew up sheltered from the many temptations of city life and what he described as 'the fleshpots of Native Africa' that surrounded his boyhood home in the section of Freetown known as Kossoh Town.[14] His recollections are filled with the warmth of memorable events and people and he fondly recalls Daddy Ali, the Muslim Temne chief who lived on his street, and the wonderful festivals held in his compound during the evenings of Ramadan. These, he tells us, reached a climax at the end of the month with 'mammoth feasting and a carnival procession of magic lanterns and paper objects in the form of ships, railways, giant dolls and charades'.[15] While apparently a Muslim tradition in Freetown during Cole's youth, 'Lanterns' has grown over the years into a truly urban phenomenon. Today it embraces all sectors of the city, Christian and traditionalist as well as Muslim, and its elaborate floats and masquerades, while including the subject matter of Islam, are grand reflections of the diversity of Freetown life.[16]

While the secular nature of contemporary Freetown Lantern processions strikes the viewer most forcibly, its Muslim roots, maintained by its timing at the end of Ramadan and the appearance of grand illuminated floats of mosques, saints' tombs and figures of Muhammad's daughter Fatima and Islamic holy men, is still very apparent.[17] One of the most striking images in 'Lanterns' is a masquerader depicting a beautiful woman surmounted by the figure of al-Burāq. A particularly stunning example was documented and photographed by Nunley in January 1978 at a parade held at Victoria Gardens in Freetown (Plate 60). Built by the highly regarded Temne artist Amara Kamara, it fully captures the grace and majesty of this winged being.[18] To produce this elegant masked character, Kamara combined a rich assortment of imported cloth, locally produced wax resist cotton prints, carved and painted wooden faces, synthetic materials, wire mesh and strips of heavy lace fringe reminiscent of the detail on Victorian gowns. Kamara's al-Burāq is a product of urban consumption brought together and shaped by an urban imagination.

An examination of this masked being quickly reveals the artistry at play. Al-Burāq is carried by a male dancer impersonating a well endowed and beautiful woman. The carved mask he wears is a strident pink and is highlighted by facial features outlined in black; five-pointed stars are painted in white upon the forehead and cheeks of the mask, surrounded by black crosses and short parallel marks; bright yellow has been applied to the upper eyelids. The hairstyle consists of tresses and generous lobes, carefully carved and painted black with white highlights. At the ears are large black and white earrings. Her body is covered with a startling combination of colours: green and yellow cloth envelop the upper torso and legs; a vivid orange brassière is enlivened with blue and white dots and a blue and white cloth with the image of Queen Elizabeth II wearing a crown is wrapped around the waist; white gloves and high white socks are on her hands and feet; and a long white train trails from her back and is held respectfully by two young women acting as bridesmaids.

Perched atop this remarkable figure is al-Burāq, captured by Kamara as if she were in flight. She is also conceived as an image of ideal womanhood but her beauty is of a very different kind, and indeed of a very different world. Kamara painted her skin a creamy yellow, gave her flowing black hair and facial features including the aquiline nose and dark almond-shaped eyes that for him capture the sultry Semitic look appropriate to al-Burāq: her colouring, facial features, hair and overall exotic allure are remarkably close to the images of al-Burāq found in North African prints. That Kamara was most likely drawn to and profoundly influenced by such works is reinforced by yet other details. The large, vaulted crown topped by a crescent shape to which is tied two handkerchiefs is a virtual restating of the plumed crown worn by al-Burāq in these popular North African depictions. Her wings, a combination of long slender feathers and a short spotted variety, both enhanced by lace trimming, are hallmarks of the winged al-Burāq in mass-produced images and have been rendered fully and with consummate patience and artistry by Kamara. The heavy jewellery which she normally wears appears around her neck, but unable to attach the pentacle upon the pendant he simply painted it, indeed several times, upon the face mask worn by the dancer. In motion this sculptural version of al-Burāq, with airy wings and flowing handkerchiefs, fully captures the essence of this mystical steed.

**60**

Amara Kamara's mask of al-Buraq worn in a parade at Victoria Gardens in Freetown, Sierra Leone, January 1978. Highly effective synthetic materials, lace, imported cloth and paint have been combined to create this urban rendition of the mystical winged horse.
Photography courtesy of John W. Nunley.

Two further examples of the winged horse, remarkably different in character, reveal how this transcendent being has insinuated itself into the artistic life of another African society. The two images were fashioned by the Baga of coastal Guinea, a people still largely non-Muslim but increasingly touched by the influence of Islam. The first is a large polychrome caryatid drum housed in the Musée de L'Homme in Paris. It is carved from a single massive log and apparently was used within the *Simo* society, the traditional Baga male initiatory organization.[19] The drum rests upon the back of a saddled horse and just below its shoulders are two delicate wing-like shapes outlined in white. Beneath the left wing is an inscription in Roman and Arabic characters that excites the mind but is, unfortunately, unreadable. These are the only references to al-Burāq on this large and noble steed, only minor details, yet in their subtlety they may be entirely sufficient. The use of al-Burāq to support a traditional initiation drum may be difficult to appreciate but the intent is both logical and profound. It was, after all, upon the back of al-Burāq that Muhammad was transported into the highest reaches and mysteries of the seven heavens and before the majesty of God. Al-Burāq thus served as the vehicle for initiation into prophethood, and so is a perfect icon for a drum whose deep resonance would help to carry Baga boys to manhood.

An equally intriguing, but far less ambiguous, Baga interpretation of the winged steed is a wooden assemblage of sculpted and carpentered parts that is a 'promised gift' to the Museum of Cultural History at UCLA. (Plate 62) A box or stage-like construction, it incorporates three finely-shaped images of al-Burāq and is generously painted with sparkling geometric patterns. Extending from the front of the box is an impressive human head wearing a crown with a projection at its back that appears to be an attempt to render the plume associated with al-Burāq. A single band of jewellery, a necklace, is carved in relief around the neck and discreetly decorated. This dominant image has large wings issuing from the interior of the box (which must be read as the body of this large al-Burāq), compelling the viewer to recognise its powers of flight, each feather accented with its own

**61**

Subtle references to al-Burāq appear on this Baga caryatid drum. This drum rests upon a saddled horse with delicate wings and Roman and Arabic characters painted on its flank. Photograph courtesy of the Musée de L'Homme. Baga Drum. #33.40.90

**62**

A Baga puppet stage with three carved images of al-Burāq — said to have been carried at village festivals by young male dancers.

Baga, Guinea. Wood, paint. 110 cm

Promised gift to UCLA, Museum of Cultural History

colour. Extending from the back of its body is a large shape that captures the mass of upright peacock feathers seen in contemporary prints. Two miniature sculpted versions of al-Burāq accompany the large form and stand to each side of its outstretched wings. From within the body and protruding beneath it is a short wooden rod that may well have been attached to a larger pole by which the work was carried.

This wonderfully literal, sculptural statement of the Prophet's horse is the same work (with some minor changes) that appears in D.T. Niane's volume *Le Soudan Occidental au Temps des Grands Empires*, which he identified as al-Burāq.[20] Only a few details differ: the cloth apron along the base of the box-like body has been removed; one of the two smaller carvings of al-Burāq appears to have been replaced; some of the painted motifs such as those on the wooden pediment at the front of the body, or details at the top of the side panels, have been repainted. According to the author this complex construction was carried by strong young Baga dancers at village festivals and is 'a curious example of religious syncretism'.[21] Whether this sculpture was produced for Muslim or traditional festivals is not indicated by Niane, but one cannot fail to appreciate the ability of the artist, whatever his religious affiliation, to capture the cosmological essence surrounding the figure of al-Burāq. Painted with bold crescent shapes and starburst patterns, these celestial signs fully honour the transcendent and magical voyage of the remarkable steed that carried Muhammad across the seven heavens to the throne of his creator.

**63**

Within the shimmering iridescence of Yoruba indigo tie-dyed cloths (*adire*) one often finds imaginative renditions of the crowned and winged al-Buraq with peacock tail-feathers.
Yoruba, Nigeria. Indigo-dyed cotton. 195 cm
Norma Wolff

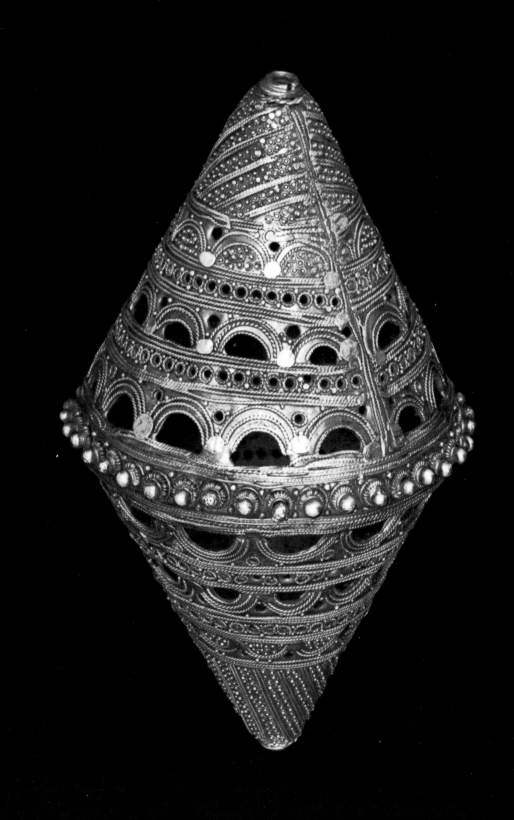

# CHAPTER SIX

# Islamic Patterns –
# a penchant for beauty
# and privacy

Images like those of al-Burāq are fascinating for they reveal the iconic potential inherent in African Islam. This is compelling imagery, capable of concentrating upon both human and natural forms and involving artists in rich iconographic adventures that easily blend Islamic and traditional African modes of perception and belief. Yet there is another face to Muslim creativity that is much more common and visible – an artistry that conspicuously avoids representation in favour of a passionate pursuit of elegant shapes, complex geometric patterns, sumptuous colours and exquisite textures. To look at such objects is to confront a world of forms marked by a special beauty and purity of design that cannot fail to please the beholder. These are mostly humble items – cushions, robes, textiles, baskets and jewellery – the things we term the 'minor arts'. Yet they are so consummately crafted, so thoroughly ennobled, that they clamour for our attention.

The preference for beautifying the surface of things is not confined to African Islam, but is a recurring and universal feature of the faith. Muslims everywhere have always fashioned their monuments and objects with an eye for pattern, the organizing principles of geometry and a fondness for the repetition of motifs. Of course, decoration is common to the visual language of all cultures, for people cannot do without it, but only within Islam does it become such a dominant expressive mode and an end in itself. The reasons for this have long been debated, the arguments ranging from the purely theological to those concerned with the psychological aspects of Islamic civilization.[1] The most persistent and compelling explanation, perhaps, is well expressed by Oleg Grabar and revolves about the very nature of the religion and its attitude towards the arts:

> The faith itself imposed restrictions on artistic creativity. Representations of living things are not prohibited *expressis verbis* by the Koran, but much in the Revelation – its opposition to idols, its monotheism, its profound sense of God as the unique Agent – argues against specificity of iconographic meanings.[2]

Religious dogma and theological opinion consistently rejected imagery as a suitable and valid avenue for the artistic imagination and were uncompromising in their condemnation of artists who sought to work in this vein. Such individuals are described in the orthodox literature by the Arabic term *musawwir*, meaning 'creator' or 'fashioner', a word with multiple references that in the Koran is reserved exclusively for Allah, the true creator, and is therefore regarded as blasphemous when applied to man. The creation of images is unlawful, an intrusion into God's domain, and is thus considered to be an act of supreme arrogance: artists who pursue this practice, it is said, will be punished by God and his prophet on the day of judgement. That the full weight of orthodox authority has been ignored, even flaunted, can be seen throughout the history of the faith, particularly in the monuments in all Muslim lands. Yet these stringent proscriptions did have a profound effect, for they fostered a particular outlook, a cast of mind and sensibility that was to encourage the special delight for surface decoration that has come to characterize the arts of Islam.

**64 (title page)**

Large filigree bead worn by Wolof and Fulani women. The gold washing of silver-copper alloys is a hallmark of Wolof jewellery and is here richly combined with filigree and granulation technique.
Wolof, Senegal. Silver-copper alloy, gold-washed
Harrison Eiteljorg Collection

**65**

Collected at Oyo in 1951 by the late William Bascom, this leather hassock demonstrates the organizing powers of geometric design and the strong desire for the rotation of shapes, in this instance squares and interlace patterns.
Oyo Yoruba, Nigeria. Dyed leather. 195 cm
Lowie Museum of Anthropology, University of California, Berkeley. #5-11847

**66**

A Nupe stool whose seat has been fully subjected to the rhythms of geometry: a reflected square, intersected by a bold crossing pattern, is surrounded by bands containing half-moon and diamond shapes.
Nupe. Bida, Nigeria. Wood. 29 cm
Collection of Arnold Rubin

**65**

**66**

**67**
Rosettes, diamonds, and chevron patterns created with seeds and beads appear with measured regularity upon this lidded basket of dyed and natural grass fibres from Somali.
Somalia. Grass, glass, beads, seeds.
50 cm
Museum of the Philadelphia Civic Center. 1900.1.239 a & b

It has never been denied that the iconoclastic attitudes of official Islam directed the energies of its artists away from the world of imagery and representation and turned them towards the realms of abstraction and ornamentation. However, other opinions have been proferred in an attempt to explain this particular creative bent. Richard Ettinghausen suggests that even without such stringent religious prohibitions Muslim artistry would have followed the same course, for he believes there is something inherent in the Muslim character that would lead artists towards what he described as the 'decorative urge'.[3] Muslim artists, he writes, are predisposed towards abstraction, as if drawn by some deep psychic force to the creation of pattern. Thus, when referring to the world about them for inspiration, they invariably reduce and reshape its natural forms into delightfully complex configurations of pure design. In the hands of Muslim artists even the shapes of leaves became 'so stylized as to be barely recognizable'.[4]

To attribute the essence of a civilization's artistic style to a 'natural instinct', as Ettinghausen does, is to tread on dangerous ground. But he

**68**

A Nupe brass bowl with fluted
lid reveals the love of geometry
and pattern in African Islamic
artistry.
Nupe, Nigeria. Brass. 22 cm
Private collection

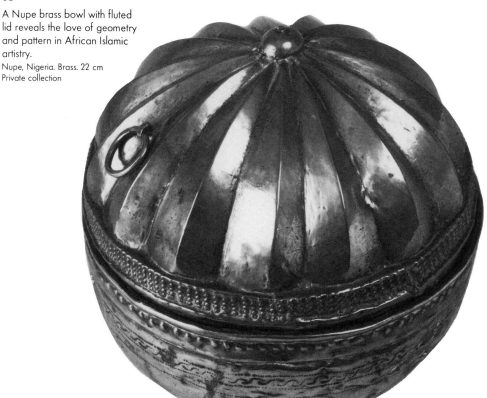

has other theories that may well help to explain the Muslim 'decorative
urge'. For Ettinghausen, the love of colour and ornamentation also stems
from a human and creative response to the natural environment over
which Islam found itself triumphant.

> A great deal of the landscape is barren, of a single dull colour and unusually
> devoid of striking features. The main elements of nearly every region are
> deserts, treeless mountains and the unrelieved monotony of infinite
> vistas . . .[5]

Villages and cities share this overall monotony, for they are built of
earthen bricks, sun-dried or baked, and local sandstones. Colour and
pattern are applied to objects and architecture as if to separate them
visually and psychologically from their surroundings. In the process these
man-made forms 'were tamed and cultivated and . . . also made en-
joyable'.[6]

The triumph of the decorative over the representational, according to
Ettinghausen, was assured by several unifying features and 'interacting

**69**

The inscription of lidded brass containers (kuduos), with the patterns and calligraphic lines reminiscent of Arabic script, is a tradition of prestige artistry among the Asante of Ghana.
Asante, Ghana. 16.5 cm
Metropolitan Museum of Art, Michael C. Rockefeller Memorial Collection, gift of Nelson A. Rockefeller, 1964. #1978.412.386 a, b

**70**

Sheet brass container with floral, tendril, and geometric motifs perhaps inspired by Sudanic and Saharan textile and leather-working traditions.
Akan (?), Ghana. Brass. 53.5 cm
Field Museum of Natural History. #89839

**71**

Mauretanian women keep their jewellery and valuables in small wooden boxes (sandoug likbir) overlayed with patterns of sheet brass, copper and, more rarely, silver.
Moors, Mauretania. Wood, brass, copper, silver. 32 cm
American Museum of Natural History. #90.2/5139

**72**

Shapely leather water containers with pouring and filling spouts and ivory and bone stoppers, are found among the Beja Bedouins of the Republic of Sudan, and as far south as the Galla and Amhara of Ethiopia. The 'decorative urge' is reserved in this instance to the elegant leather strap.

UCLA, Museum of Cultural History, gift of the Wellcome Trust. X67-554

conditions' within Islam itself. As a religious culture Islam inculcated among its diverse believers a strong sense of community, influencing the arts 'by creating a way of life and general attitudes that were to become universally accepted'.[7] It forged a vast economic network that linked Muslims in Spain and Africa with those on the Asian sub-continent. Artists moved along the trade routes, taking with them their ideas and techniques, and the creative products of an entire civilization.[8] A language of abstract decoration developed and spread quickly to all parts of the Islamic world, becoming a hallmark of Muslim creativity.[9]

Another source of inspiration that has been suggested for this fascination with pattern and design is the highly refined world of Islamic mathematics and geometry. I find this particularly compelling for art and mathematics have so much in common. Both fields of creativity demand clarity of vision, precision of thought and considerable organizing capabilities. If 'calculation was an endless delight' for the mathematician, the artist revelled in what appeared to be the infinite possibilities of shapes and patterns.[10] Not only were their methods and dispositions akin but, as has been suggested, within Islamic civilization the artist and mathematician literally became one.[11] Artists achieved a beauty and intricacy of visual pattern that required a full understanding of the rules and regularities of geometry including 'highly complex number theories and elaborate developments of rotation, symmetry and transformation'.[12]

How to interpret and understand this exquisite wealth of geometric pattern is another matter. The complexity of forms, the symmetries of their rotation and reflection, and the wonderful interplay of light and dark shapes are enchanting and a constant source of pleasure and satisfaction. They may be enjoyed simply for their beauty and this is how they have often been treated, but as Grabar suggests, 'it may not be correct to interpret this ornamentation as a purely arbitrary exercise in design, whose only objective would have been the beautification of the surface on which it occurs'.[13] Others have seen this world of precise pattern as a mirror of far deeper realities, as artistry reflecting the unseen rhythms and laws inherent in God's creation and guiding will. Such consummate craftsmanship therefore occurs in the world to remind man of his deeper and more enduring relationship to the cosmos, as a reflection of the metaphysical and cosmological dimensions of Islam. Such interpretations are appealing for they ask us to consider the possibility of 'geometry as a metaphor for the all pervasive but intangible divine, for the presence of God . . . the endless variations in the same geometric forms as the visual version of the names of God so common in Muslim piety'.[14] Yet such analysis may go too far, presuming too direct a relationship between the mystical and esoteric realms and the expressive intent of this geometric decoration.

It is also possible to see this 'decorative urge' as stemming from qualitative features within Muslim life and among its believers. The relationships between the desire for abstract patterning and ideas concerning personal privacy and the ways in which Muslims present themselves and interact with one another are both subtle and indirect. Yet

**73**

The Islamic architecture of Djenne, and specifically the relief wall designs of small rural mosques in the region outside of the town, can be seen in the window-like openings and decorative edges on the sides of this stool.

Djenne, Mali. Wood. 53 cm
University Museum, University of Pennsylvania. #72-31-2

I feel they do exist. To spend any time in a Muslim community in Africa is to become acutely aware that one has entered a very distinct environment, one that is essentially different from a traditional or Christian setting. There are, of course, the obvious differences, certain sights and sounds immediately discernable as Islamic: the mosque, the manner of dress, the melodies of prayer and everyday speech, laced with references to Allah and his many attributes. Other features that are part of the tenor of existence require more time to appreciate, and include the subdued quality of personal interactions, the stateliness and dignity with which individuals carry themselves, and a strong desire for privacy. Life in general is much more private than in traditional and Christian communities, and this is assured by styles of domestic architecture that are oriented not to the outside world, but towards a set of interior spaces and courtyards. Women, so prominent and obvious a force in traditional African life, are more sheltered and men seem to carry on their affairs with a degree of reserve that is impressive. There is an overall tone to a Muslim society that is muted and pervaded by an air of grace and refinement of manners which lends discretion and quiet elegance to life.

**74**

Scrolls and diamonds are brought together in this cushion originally exhibited at the Exposition Universelle de Paris in 1900.
People's Republic of Benin. Leather, cotton.
Museum of the Philadelphia Civic Center.
#1900.1.202

**75**

A hint of the possible influence of Islamic design is seen in the interlace patterns of leather appliqué upon this Benin fan.
Benin, Nigeria. Leather, textile, wood. 62 cm
UCLA, Museum of Cultural History, gift of the Wellcome Trust. #X-65-9007

It is in such communities that the Muslim desire for decoration abounds, and it is fascinating. My initial response to Muslim artistry was one of surprise because it seemed so out of place: here were objects that flaunted their beauty, while the people who made and used them appeared so sombre. The contrast was striking and I wondered if the objects had been given this surface beauty to compensate for the restraint so evident among the people. However, I came to realize that these things were most appropriate to their setting and in fact very much like their owners. Most of them – the stools, elegant calabashes, ceramic containers, cushions and chests – were intensely personal items meant to grace the lives of those who possessed them and to be enjoyed in the privacy of their homes. Elaborate gowns and cloths, while beautiful to behold, were created with such fullness that the body invariably remained hidden; surface patterns that at first appeared so spontaneous were in fact carefully planned and executed, sharing a level of refinement and formality found in the human sphere. Decorative patterns, like formal gestures and manners, occur on the surface, revealing little while concealing a great deal.

76

**76**

A lavishly embroidered full-length man's gown (*riga*) from the important Hausa city of Kano in northern Nigeria. Eyelet stitching makes visible the repetitive pattern of circles and the large square border that surrounds the chest panel containing a square of five circles across and five down.

Hausa, Nigeria. Cotton, silk. 255 cm

Metropolitan Museum of Art, Michael Rockefeller Memorial Collection. #1979.206.279

**77**

This Dogon stool is strongly influenced by the patterns and geometric precision of Islam. The centre of the seat and the sides of the stool have been generously pierced to allow for the play of light upon the chevron, triangular, interlace and five-square patterns.

Dogon, Mali. Wood. 41 cm

American Museum of Natural History. #90.2.3539

The penchant in Islam for privacy, for shielding so much of itself and its believers from the public eye, is surely what has inspired the styles of clothing within this civilization. Islam consistently encourages habits of modesty and propriety, and this is well illustrated by the voluminous, full-length men's gowns of the Hausa of northern Nigeria; known as *rigas*, they are worn over sleeveless smocks and cotton trousers. A particularly splendid *riga*, in the collection of the Metropolitan Museum of Art, comes from the important city of Kano and is made of white cotton enhanced with embroidered panels of natural silk.[15] (Plate 76) Its splendour suggests that it was worn by a man of substance and reserved for special occasions – Friday mosque services or major holidays, like the small and great *Sallah*, held at the end of Ramadan and on *Id al-Kabir*. Some two-and-a-half metres wide, it would completely envelop and conceal the body of its owner in folds of cloth, proudly proclaiming his membership within the community of the faithful.

While effectively hiding the body, this particular *riga* would also call attention to itself and to the man who wore it, for the surface embroidery is beautiful, yet so subtle and intricate that to fully appreciate it requires concentrated attention. The selection of a creamy silk for the embroidered portions of the white cloth suggests a desire for a subtle garment; modulation of surface and colour is achieved by an eyelet embroidery technique that results in a denser surface and a slightly deeper cream tone. The eyelet stitch makes visible the repetitive pattern of circles, the lines connecting them and the large square border that surrounds the chest panel containing a square measuring five circles across and five down. Like the Hausa men of character who wear them, who are said to prefer white gowns with subtle tones of embroidery to more colourful and strident garments, this work is imbued with an inner glow and excellence of being. Its special radiance, like that of the good man in Hausa culture, warms the heart and is readily felt and appreciated.[16]

**78**

The desire to beautify the surfaces of things that cover and conceal is also observable in a shuttered wooden window and grille decorated with brass from a home in Timbuktu. (Plate 78) Houses in Timbuktu, as in many towns of the Niger bend, are two-storeyed, rectangular, mud-brick fortresses with solid walls, buttressed at regular intervals and to either side of a single doorway. What impresses the viewer is their unrelenting walls of mud that shut out the world and hide the life contained within them. To walk in the narrow streets of Timbuktu, according to Miner, is to move along paths 'bordered by the continuous walls of dwellings'.[17] Only an occasional wooden door, at times embossed and studded with finely-forged geometric iron shapes and knockers, announces the presence of a home. High up, at second-storey level, are small openings cut into the wall and filled with shuttered, grilled windows known locally as *soro funey*. The single door and these small windows are all that relieve the monotony of the mud walls — the only spots through which light and sound may penetrate their monolithic character.[18]

The grilled windows are shapely apertures that permit light and sometimes a cooling breeze into the upper storey rooms. Their placement high on the walls and their screen-like construction assures privacy even when the shutters are fully open. In the evenings the shutters are closed to block out the chill night air and to keep away the jinn, those spirits that are said to roam freely in the darkness. Full window grilles without shutters are a common feature of North African domestic architecture, where they are known as *mashrabiyya*, and their appearance in Timbuktu is both a legacy and a reminder of the sixteenth-century Moroccan conquest of the Niger delta. According to Miner, Timbuktu window grilles are based upon Moroccan designs; there is certainly a strong visual relationship between the two traditions. Like the Moroccan ones those from Timbuktu (where the grille portion covers only the bottom half of the window) are carpentered screens of flat wooden slats (unlike those seen in Egypt, which are made from turned pieces of wood) joined together in lattice fashion, with an eye for bold geometric pattern.

The shuttered window with a partial screen from Timbuktu in the Van Gilder collection exhibits most of the features commonly found in *soro funey* from the Niger delta. The upper half of the window consists of an arched opening, the lower half contains the lattice screen and there are two full-length shutters. The slats in the screen have been cut and joined to form star patterns. Three full star octagons (created by superimposing a square rotated forty-five degrees upon another square) occur in the middle row of the screen and are bounded on all sides by star-like patterns of three and five points. The same star octagon is the dominant motif in many Moroccan *mashrabiyya*, where the interior of the star is filled with extremely delicate lattice work, but in the Van Gilder piece and others from Timbuktu the star is left open. A number of details on this window are specifically local in character and do not appear in Moroccan examples. Small brass discs are discreetly applied at regular intervals along the entire frame of the window and in the same rhythmic manner on the slats which comprise the grille, and on the jamb where the shutters meet. On the shutters themselves are finely-cut brass rectangles with tendrils at the corners and two metal bosses edged with starburst patterns. Most unusual, is a gracefully stylized rendering of the Arabic letter *waw*, incised all over the four edges of the window frames and on the cross-piece at the top of the grille. One of the many symbols of Allah, the letter *waw* strengthens the structural elements of this window, metaphorically filling it with his presence. A massive and undifferentiated mud wall was once graced by this skilled example of the work of a carpenter and a metalworker, and with the creator himself.

**78**

Shuttered and grilled wooden windows (*soro funey*) in the area of the Niger bend are a legacy of the sixteenth century Moroccan conquest of this region. This example from Timbuktu, with a grille design based upon the star octagon pattern, is reminiscent of Moroccan grilles (*mashrabiyya*) where the same motif occurs with great frequency.
Songhai. Timbuktu, Mali. Wood, metal. 96.5 cm
Collection of Edmund & Lilliana Van Gilder

I shall conclude this brief look at the surface beauty of Muslim artistry by turning to three objects crafted in very different media. The first is an elegant ceramic Nupe waterpot from Bida, Nigeria in the collection of the National Museum of African Art.[19] Although of a standard Nupe form, it is beautifully enhanced with metal appliqué that surrounds its mouth, neck and shoulders like pieces of fine jewellery. (Plate 79) A second example is a large, round, broad-brimmed hat with conical crown acquired by the old Philadelphia Commercial Museum (now the Museum of the Philadelphia Civic Center) in 1894, provisionally attributed to the Bassa of Liberia.[20] It is made of coiled and woven grasses, a layer of broad-leafed grass, and natural fibres. (Plate 80) The third object, a round Senegalese leather cushion, is most likely the work

**79**

Nupe ceramic water container with metal appliqué surrounding the mouth, neck, and shoulders like pieces of fine jewellery. Triangles, circles and bosses form the dominant appliqué patterns.
Nupe, Nigeria. Terracotta, metal. 41 cm
National Museum of African Art, Smithsonian Institution. #82.6.2

**80**

The brim of this Liberian hat has a twelve-fold double row of open triangles. Their number and regularity recall the Zodiac and the rhythms of the lunar year.
Bassa (?), Liberia. Most likely Fulbe and possibly from Guinea. Broad leaf grasses, fibres. 58.5 cm
Museum of the Philadelphia Civic Center. #1894.1.6

79

of a Mauretanian leatherworker, a member of the artisan class known as *mallemin*, and was purchased by the same museum in 1900 at the *Exposition Universelle* in Paris.[21] It is a lovely cushion consisting of triangular shapes sewn together with strong blue-and-white cord and short leather fringing where the top and bottom are sewn to each other. (Plate 81)

What is so appealing in each of these pieces is their carefully planned beauty. All three are finely-crafted forms that combine the artist's intimate feeling for materials with the organizing possibilities and patterns of geometry. Each piece is an excursion into the qualities and potential of circles and triangles and the many ramifications and relationships that exist between them.

On the Liberian hat are guiding circles; one formed by the base of the crown, three on the brim passing through the twelve diamonds that encircle the crown, a fifth created by the edge of the generous brim itself. The five form a set of embracing circles that enabled the weaver to create a twelve-fold double row of open triangles, the two rows staggered just enough to create twelve perfectly equivalent diamonds. Their number and spatial regularity recall the Zodiac and recurrent rhythms of the lunar year. In the Mauretanian leather cushion a perfect sixteen-fold flowering of the circle, resulting in sixteen equivalent triangles, is sewn together to form a beautifully balanced eight-pointed star. The round body of the Nupe ceramic vessel is equally subject to considerations of geometric design. The metal appliqué is highlighted by triangles, individual circles and clusters of three circles and dots: four sets of three round bosses arranged in an inverted triangle pattern are spread equally about the shoulder of the pot; between them are four upright triangles, each inscribed with a circle, three sets of three clustered dots and two smaller inscribed triangles; small circles and the same cluster of three dots are also found upon the appliqué neck and lip of the pot. Circles and triangles distinguish this metal appliqué and their occurrence in groups of three, four and its several multiples is indeed striking. Distributed with geometric precision, these metallic patterns not only grace the Nupe vessel with beauty but suggest levels of thought that may well touch upon Islamic notions of the cosmos and the sanctity of visual order and repetition.

**81**

A Mauretanian leather cushion with a perfect sixteen-fold flowering of the circle, (resulting in sixteen equivalent triangles) is sewn together to form a balanced eight-point star.

Mauretania. Leather, blue-and-white cord. 41 cm
Museum of the Philadelphia Civic Center.
#1900.1.197

82

# CHAPTER SEVEN

# The Swahili Coast –
# a bazaar of forms and styles

I want to conclude this set of reflections on the artistry of African Islam by turning to the continent's eastern coast and Swahili civilization, where a profound synthesis of Bantu Africa and Islam has taken place over a period of at least ten centuries. On the Swahili coast Islam and Africa have long lived closely with one another and a special style has been created there which is both unique and enduring. The very language instantly directs us to the character of Swahili culture. Spoken Swahili is an artful blend, an intermingling of Arab and Bantu elements that can be heard by the most casual traveller. Its vocabulary is drawn in almost equal proportions from each language, but much of its Arabic vocabulary has been absorbed phonetically and adapted to Bantu rules of grammar. Its syntax, the rhythmic basis of Swahili, combines the metric properties of both languages and reflects fully the heartbeat of this people. Swahili literature, with roots going back to at least the late seventeenth century, is written in a modified Arabic script and includes an impressive body of proverbs, verse, and prose that combines Bantu wisdom with the spirit and substance of Islam. 'The Koran, the legends of the Prophet Muhammad and the other prophets and saints . . . points of doctrine and theology are referred to on every page of traditional Swahili literature.'[1] While deeply influenced by currents from the southern Arabian peninsula and other portions of the Indian Ocean, the Swahili world is not simply a pale reflection of Arab and Islamic civilization: it is something that is decidedly different, an important culture with its own identity and style.

Swahili civilization was born out of the intercourse of coastal peoples with Muslim Arab, Persian and, later in its history, Indian or Malabar merchants. Its people were and are townspeople, although never exclusively so, and its history has been intimately tied to the rising and falling fortunes of trading towns: Manda, in the Lamu archipelago, achieved its height in the twelfth century; medieval prosperity was evident in the ports of Mogadishu, Kilwa and Mombasa; Lamu and Zanzibar reached economic prominence in the nineteenth century. Swahili towns have always consisted of stone and coral houses enhanced with beautifully carved doors and intricate plasterwork and have been graced by shapely mosques and impressive monumental tombs. Islam shaped the religious and commercial life of these communities, it influenced people's conduct and helped set the tone for life itself. The African component within Swahili life, however, has always been present. It is to be found in the language itself and it forms the basis of Swahili stone architecture, whose form and style (and its use of mangrove roof beams) developed out of local mud and wattle traditions. African religious notions concerning ancestors, spirit possession and witchcraft were incorporated into Swahili beliefs and coexist everywhere in Islam.

Nothing brings home the special character of this Muslim civilization quite as dramatically as Swahili artistry. Swahili art and architecture are the product of a particular state of mind and being, of creativity that is firmly based upon culture and religion. The arts were, and are, conceived and shaped within the urban environment, and while not exclusively a

**82 (title page)**

Nineteenth-century Zanzibar door in the late 'Indianized Style'. Carving is shallow and curvilinear, floral motifs predominate and there is a degree of realism that is atypical of Swahili craftsmanship.
Photograph courtesy of Mr Robert Nooter

**83**

A lavishly embroidered Swahili man's cap (kofia) acquired at the end of the nineteenth century in the eastern province of the Belgian Congo. The dating suggests that aspects of Swahili culture were beginning to appear in precisely those areas that were gradually being opened up and settled by Swahili merchants during this period.
Swahili hat. Cotton, cotton embroidery thread. 26 cm
American Museum of Natural History

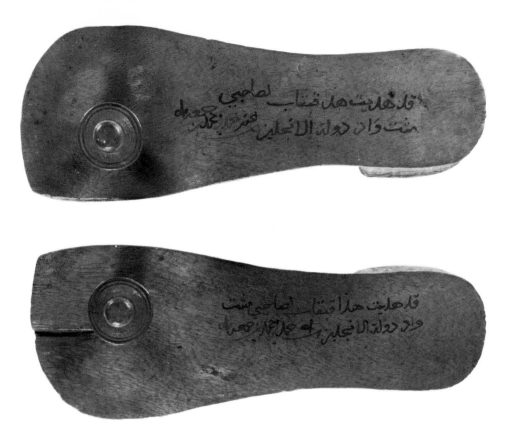

phenomenon of town life, their fullest flowering surely stems from this
setting. Artistry is an important part of the very definition of Swahili
culture for, in the words of James de Vere Allen, the Swahili themselves
stress that culture can only flourish in towns and is indeed the
'prerogative of townsmen'. To the Swahili, 'culture is interpreted as a
social patina, a way of life and knowledge of how to behave which can
only be learned, indeed can only be practised, by those living in towns . . .'[2]
The very words for culture in Swahili, Allen tells us, reinforce these
thoughts: *utamaduni*, derives from the Arabic root medina or town; *usta-
arabu*, 'behaving like an Arab' refers to urban modes of conduct.
*U-ungwana*, the oldest Swahili term for culture, has many meanings,
ranging from 'someone who has the freedom of the city' to a 'man of good
breeding and taste', but is most fully expressed as 'the quintessence of
Swahili-ness'.[3] The most visible expressions of Swahili identity and
culture are surely its objects and monuments, created with a sense of style
and a level of refinement that is stunning.

   The arts not only help to define Swahili civilization but remind us, in the
clearest way possible, of the nature and rhythms of its history. To look at
this artistry is to recognize quickly that the Swahili are the product of many

**84**

'I have presented these clogs to
my friend Mister Ward, English
Govn't,' signed Hamed bin
Muhammad. A token of
friendship from the famous Arab
Zanzibari trader Tippu Tip (born
Hamed bin Muhammed al
Murjebi) to the English artist and
adventurer Herbert Ward, circa
1890.
Swahili. Wood, ink. 28 cm
National Museum of Natural History,
Smithsonian Institution. #323.366

different peoples and events, forged, over the last thousand years, along the East African coast and its off-shore islands, from Warsheikh in southern Somalia to the border of Mozambique. The influences are numerous, coming from the interior of East Africa, the coast itself, and from as far afield as the Arabian Peninsula, the Persian Gulf, India and southeast Asia. That the coastal Swahili have always looked seaward, that they have long been a part of a larger western Indian Ocean civilization has certainly been recognized. Less apparent, but surely as important, is the fact that the Swahili are very much 'themselves', a people firmly rooted on African soil. Swahili history is a blending of Africa and Asia, a result of the meeting of peoples and ideas from abroad with those of the East Africa coast, and the 'special genius' of this culture, as Allen put it, has always been its ability to absorb these many influences, to 'Swahili-ize them', while retaining its own identity.[4] This too forms part of the character of Swahili creativity.

**85**

A prayer mat (*mswala*), woven by a Pokomo woman from the Tana River district of the northern Kenya Coast, demonstrates the convergence of certain non-Swahili African motifs with Swahili shapes.
Pokomo, Kenya. Dyed and natural grasses. 253 cm
Museum of the Philadelphia Civic Center. No. cat. #

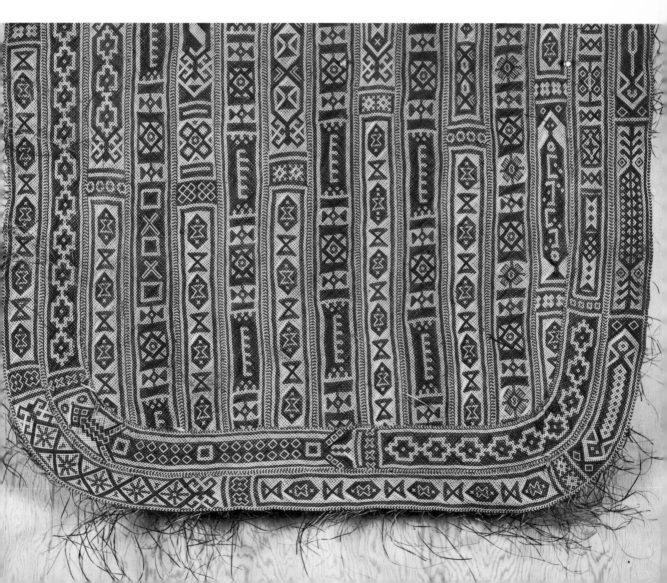

**86**

The *kita cha enzi*, an exercise in angularity, is a marvellous Swahili
improvisation upon a nineteenth-century Anglo-Indian chair.
Swahili. Lamu, Kenya. Wood, string. 123 cm
National Museum of Natural History, Smithsonian Institution. #409.943

An example of Swahili craftsmanship that reveals much of the culture's character and history is a large high back ebony chair with arms and a footrest, that is generously inlaid with delicate ivory and bone designs and includes panels of string or fibre. (Collection of the National Museum of Natural History, Smithsonian Institution.)[5] (Plate 86) Collected at the town of Lamu, on Lamu Island just off the northern Kenya coast, it is a recent version of the *kita cha enzi*, a nineteenth century chair popular in Lamu and further south at Mombasa and on the island of Zanzibar. *Kita cha enzi* means literally 'chair of power', and such chairs are among the few items of furniture found in Swahili homes.[6] The *kita cha enzi* is an exercise in angularity – square in shape and dominated by 45 degree angles. It is a tall chair but is extremely shallow in order to fit within the narrow spaces of Swahili rooms. While these are features of all Swahili chairs, what distinguishes the *kita cha enzi* is the use of ebony, the lavish additions of bone and ivory inlay, elaborate string or coconut fibre panels (reminiscent of caning) found on the back, sides and footrest, and the fact each has a removable back. It's name may also be translated as 'Grandee's chair', a wonderfully apt title that honours both the craftsman and the wealthy urban owner of this most noble and refined throne,

I find the *kita cha enzi* intriguing, as so little is known about its origins and history. Allen who is surely the leading interpreter of Swahili culture, regarded it as a purely East African creation inspired by earlier eighteenth-century Swahili chairs, of a similar square and angular style, solidly built out of a local hardwood known as *mtwanda*. At first, these were minimally decorated with incised grooves and herring-bone designs and occasionally inlaid, although rather simply, with bone, ebony or some other wood, and silver. Later in the century the *mtwanda* chair, and its restrained decorative surfaces, underwent a considerable transformation – '. . . simple grooving and inlay are replaced by a variety of carved holes and decorative excisions in the chairs; a process which reaches its logical conclusion in Lamu and Zanzibar in the nineteenth century with the emergence of a new variation, the *Kita cha enzi* . . .'.[8] This progression seems simple enough – ebony replaces *mtwanda*, the holes and excisions are translated and enlarged into open

fibre and string panels, and the throne is heightened and made to sparkle with the richness of elaborate ivory and bone inlay. The dynamic behind these changes, however, is purely internal, being generated by the many currents within nineteenth-century Swahili history.

Allen's analysis is certainly appealing for it is both stylistically plausible and honours the creative impulses within Swahili culture. I find his schema, however, a bit too simply drawn, especially because it does not consider the strong likelihood that the *kita cha enzi* and its eighteenth-century predecessors may ultimately derive from sources outside the Swahili world. Both are highly reminiscent of European chairs, specifically of examples from the late Queen Anne, Regency and Victorian periods, but they have undergone a most remarkable transformation. While a direct link between these Swahili chairs and such European models is quite unlikely, there was a tradition of British colonial furniture, known as the Campaign Style, which flourished in eighteenth- and nineteenth-century India and might well have served as a source of inspiration. Anglo-Indian furniture, based upon the most popular metropolitan styles, was fashioned in India from the late eighteenth century and throughout the nineteenth century for British families in the service of the East India Company, and after 1858, for soldiers and administrators of the Crown Colony. Campaign Style furniture was basically a simplified, more heavily scaled and highly functional adaptation of popular British examples. Chairs were high backed, square in their overall design, had arms and footrests, and were invariably caned; some were even elaborated with inlays of wood, shell or ivory, much like the maquetry found on Queen Anne chairs. Made of teak, rosewood and shisham, these caned chairs were remarkably well suited to the heat and humidity of India and many, because they could be folded or easily broken down, were highly portable.

The parallels between Anglo-Indian Campaign Style chairs and the *kita cha enzi* (and earlier Swahili examples) are simply too numerous to ignore. Their overall shape, general proportions, stolidity, and certain details such as maquetry and string or fibre-like caning, are unquestionably similar. Since Indian furniture is known to have been imported in considerable quantities to the Swahili coast in the

87

88

eighteenth and nineteenth centuries, especially beds and chairs from Bombay and the Malabar Coast that were patterned upon European prototypes, it is more than likely that Campaign Chairs, or copies of them were included. To suggest that the *kita cha enzi* was inspired by such an imported model is to not only acknowledge the historical realities of the Swahili world but to honour its creative sensibilities. The *kita cha enzi* is certainly not a copy of a Campaign Chair but may be a marvellous Swahili improvisation upon an Anglo-Indian furniture style. In the hands of a Swahili craftsman the Campaign Chair is turned into a throne – it becomes more massive, more angular, taller and more shallow, and is fashioned from rich ebony highlighted by glowing and repetitive ivory inlay and with white string panelling. A colonial bureaucrat's chair submitted to Indianizing influences has thus been further transformed, 'Swahilized', into a noble seat for a Grandee.

The high level of aesthetic self-confidence that has marked Swahili society is also seen in many other objects welcomed into this culture and then reshaped by local sensibilities. New techniques and tools were culturally absorbed, such as lacwork (a vegetable dyeing technique resembling lacquer painting) and the use of the wood lathe, and these further encouraged Swahili creativity. Two objects, also in the National Museum of Natural History collection, a small wooden box from the Lamu region and a cylindrical lidded container from Siyu on Fazza Island, that has been lacquered and hand painted, make these points nicely.[9]

Small and finely crafted wooden boxes, fitted with trays and containing a variety of compartments that hold writing materials, jewellery or money have long been popular in Swahili culture.[10] Used by scribes, wealthy merchants and women of substance they are especially important to this society so distinguished by its literate tradition and proud of its commercial heritage and urbanity. Made of teak, sesam, or Bombay blackwood these small boxes contain either a hasp or a small lock and are beautifully finished with sheet brass designs, incised details, metal inlay, and hardware (hinges and handles) that complement their overall elegance. The variety of boxes is dazzling: there are Surati boxes from the Gulf of Cambay to the north of Bombay; Shirazi examples from the Persian Gulf;

89

**87**

This small mortar with sliding lid, decorated in the more restrained Bajun style of the northern Swahili coast, is one example of women's household objects that are consistently enhanced and beautified through surface decoration.
Swahili, Lamu Archipelago, Kenya. Wood. 26 cm
Brooklyn Museum. #22.810

**88**

This small lathe-turned and stained cylindrical box with lid, known as *zikakasi*, is marked by a degree of grace and refinement that is a hallmark of Swahili creativity.
Swahili. Siyu, Kenya. Wood, mangrove stain. 12.5 cm
National Museum of Natural History, Smithsonian Institution. #409.947 a, b

**89**

Two flat boards are hinged in the centre to form this modern version of a traditional Koran stand (*marufad*). The upper surfaces are deeply incised with the triangles, squares, and circles within squares typical of northern Swahili decoration.
Lamu, Kenya. Wood. 52 cm, open
National Museum of Natural History, Smithsonian Institution. #409.940

highly ornate Malabar pieces with scroll carving that are made on the southwestern coast of India; and Bombay boxes with their distinctive tulip hinges and heavier brass overlay. Imported into the Swahili world with regularity, these beautiful objects, often reworked by coastal craftsmen to suit local tastes, have become an important feature of patrician life. Unlike the large brass studded chest, popularly known as *kasha la njuma* or 'box of the stars', these are intensely private and personal pieces, items that reflect the discreet confidence of their possessors. [11]

90

Imported alongside these finished boxes was a plain variety, with tray and compartments, called *kasha la mfuto*.[12] Made in Bombay and elsewhere specifically for export to the East African coast, these pieces are decorated and carefully finished by Swahili artisans and are extremely popular. A fine example of the *kasha la mfuto* is the small box from Lamu referred to above, which displays fully the restrained elegance so admired by the Swahili (Plate 90). This particular box has a sliding cover

**90**

A small wooden box, (*kasha la mfuto*), fitted with trays and several compartments for holding writing materials, jewellery or money. In its restraint and purity of lines it is typically Swahili.
Swahili. Lamu, Kenya. Wood, metal and bone. 48 cm
National Museum of Natural History, Smithsonian Institution. #409.935

**91**

A small lathe-turned lidded bowl from Siyu, stained with mangrove dyes and delicately incised.
Swahili, Siyu, Kenya. Wood. 9 cm
National Museum of Natural History, Smithsonian Institution. #409.945 a, b

91

graced with a simple brass handle and its corners, originally joined by sheet brass, have been re-worked with bone inlay. Small rounds of bone and ivory, sixteen to be exact, were added to the lid for visual interest. The top was also incised, but very simply, and five small brass discs were added in the centre and at the corners. A simple dog-tooth and cross-square pattern was incised with perfect regularity upon the three narrow trays. This box is easily distinguishable from the Indian and Persian examples that are so profusely covered with metal, and in its understatement, in the purity of its lines, is unmistakeably Swahili.

The small lathe-turned and stained cylindrical box with lid from Siyu called *zikakasi*, used for storing spices or as a cosmetic container, reveals yet another dimension of the wonderfully ab-sorptive nature of Swahili creativity (Plate 88). Siyu was, and continues to be, the most important centre for the production of these vessels but little is known about the origins of the tradition. Allen, who is very familiar with Siyu, suggests that the techniques employed derived from India where they are quite old, but there is, as he notes, 'no record of an Indian immigrant in Siyu'. He none-theless suggests that '. . . some time in the last century the people of Siyu learned the technique of turning and staining wood with mangrove dyes [mangrove trees he notes are particularly plentiful on Faza Island] as it was done in India and set themselves up as local experts in this style of woodworking'.[13] At Siyu, mangrove dyes are applied to such a box while still on the lathe and decorative motifs are added at the very end with a brush. Brightly lacquered containers are also made in India, and these dome-shaped vessels, similar to Siyu examples, are found all over the Swahili coast. They are, however, rarely enhanced with painted details and are much more densely stained. The Siyu *zikakasi* on the other hand is stained lightly and with a sombre palette of colours, and the lighter bands are covered with carefully traced geometric patterns. The stained bands are wider, its overall proportions are less globular, and its contours are remarkably subtle. Thus this *zikakasi* is also marked by a degree of grace and refinement that is very much part of the Swahili mode.

# Notes and References

## CHAPTER ONE
### A passion for the words of God

1. Clifford Geertz, 'Art as a Cultural System,' *Modern Language Notes*, vol. 91, 1976, pp. 1489–90.
2. *Ibid*, p. 1494.
3. *Ibid*, p. 1491.
4. *Ibid*, p. 1490.
5. For a discussion of the correct behaviour and bodily attitudes assumed by the faithful during the daily prayers see: G.D. Von Grunebaum, *Muhammadan Festivals* (New York: Henry Schuman, 1951) pp. 9–13. A particularly fine treatment of ritual prayer may be found in ch. 3, 'Religion and Laws' of Edward William Lane's classic study *An Account of the Manners and Customs of the Modern Egyptians*, first published in 1836.
6. Kirtsen Strandgaard, text, in J.A.R. Wembah – Rashid (ed.) *Introducing Tanzania Through the National Museum*, (Dar es Salaam: National Museum of Tanzania, 1974) p. 52.
7. I want to thank my colleagues Carol Eastman, Professor of Anthropology and Swahili, and Farhat Ziadeh, Chairman of Near Eastern Languages and Literature, for introducing me to the subject of Swahili verse written in Arabic characters. I am particularly grateful to Mr Seyed Muhammad Maulana, of Mombasa, a student in Urban Planning at the University of Washington, for deciphering sections of this extraordinary mat.
8. Dr John Hunwick, Professor of Islamic and African History, Northwestern University, kindly examined several photographed pages of this volume and it was he who recognized it as a version of the *Kitab Moussa*.
9. Arthur J. Arberry (translator), *The Koran Interpreted* (New York: Macmillan, 7th printing, 1976) p. 65.
10. This fan is one of 226 items purchased by the Field Museum from Dr Otto Finsch, Director of the Brunswick City Museum, in August 1905. All of the objects were collected by Captain Thierry in Togoland. Thierry was killed on 16 September, 1904 by Hausa or Fulani forces in a battle at Mubi in the then German Protectorate of Cameroon. The Thierry pieces are all catalogued by the Field Museum as 'Togo Hinterland Collection.' This information was kindly provided me by Dr Philip Lewis of the Field Museum and is based on an examination and translation of the correspondence between Finsch and the Museum by the late Paul Gebauer. Thanks are due to J. Hunwick for deciphering the script on the fan.
11. I am indebted to Raymond A. Silverman for information and for permission to use his field photograph of Al Hajji Abdullahi Muhammad, Imam of Techiman.
12. For a discussion of the *Tijanniya dhikr* or litany among the Hausa of Ibadan see Abner Cohen, *Custom and Politics in Urban Africa* (Berkeley: University of California Press, 1969) pp. 178–9.
13. According to William Siegmann the *Falui* is referred to by Mandingo speakers as Yoma Yoma.
14. William Siegmann and Judith Perani, 'Men's Masquerades of Sierra Leone and Liberia', *African Arts*, vol. 9, no. 3, 1976, p. 42–4.

## CHAPTER TWO
### God's secrets – shaped in silence

1. The French word *marabout* derives from the Arabic *murabit* meaning a man who is 'tied' or 'attached' to God. Used in North Africa with special reference to the cults of Sufi saints and Sufi religious brotherhoods, it is applied more generally, as it is in places like Bobo-Dioulasso (Upper Volta) and indeed throughout French-speaking West Africa, to a person of considerable religious learning, high moral character, or someone who is believed to be endowed with a special measure of holiness and grace. In other words, a marabout is someone who is seen as having a special relationship with God and whose closeness to the Divine can be communicated to others.
2. *Nassa-ji*, or 'writing water', is also referred to as holy water in Bobo-Dioulasso. One not only washes with such a solution but drinks it, for 'writing water' is considered the most intimate way to absorb God's power. *Nassa-ji* was regarded as a particularly effective protective medicine for warriors and is said to have been very popular in the late nineteenth century when the West Volta Region was initially attacked by Samory and later occupied by French colonial forces.

3. Edmond Doutté, *Magie et Religion dans l'Afrique du Nord* (Algiers: Adolphe Jourdan, 1908) pp. 150–1.

4. E.W. Lane, *An Account of the Manners and Customs of the Ancient Egyptians* (London: East-West Publications, 1978 reprint of the 1895 edn) pp. 265–6.

5. Jack Goody, 'Restricted Literacy in Northern Ghana' in J. Goody (ed.), *Literacy in Traditional Societies* (Cambridge University Press, 1968) p. 228.

6. *Ibid*.

7. The word *hatumere*, according to Labelle Prussin's notes for her exhibition 'Hatumere: Islamic Design in West Africa', is derived from the Arabic Khatam meaning 'seal' or 'signet'. In West Africa, the word is applied 'to any seal-like object with an inscription or design of a pious or religious character . . . and has evolved into a generic reference to all aspects of self-conscious design associated with Islam.' Prussin will explore this term more fully in *Hatumere: Islamic Design in West Africa*, University of California Press, soon to be released.

8. *Alfa*, a Fula or Fulbe term, is used to describe a man who has achieved a significant level of Islamic learning and is synonymous with the Malinke title *Karamoko*. According to Paul Marty, the Fula claimed that the word was an abbreviation of *Al-Fahim*, meaning wisdom or learned, but Marty felt that in fact it probably stemmed from the Manding term *Arfa* or *Arfan*, ie. chief or prince. The *Alfa*, in this sense, could be regarded as a 'prince of learning'. See P. Marty, *L'Islam en Guinée* (Paris, Ernest Laroux, 1921) p. 355. Ottenberg informs me that the term is more broadly used among the Limba where more often than not it is applied to Muslim diviners and amulet makers and teachers of the Holy Book.

9. Simon Ottenberg, 'Field Notes on Limba Art and Culture', p. 3178 dated 3–4 July, 1980.

10. Labelle Prussin, 'Hatumere: Islamic Design in West Africa', an exhibition held at the Seattle Art Museum, 30 September – 28 November 1982.

11. A.D.H. Bivar and M. Hiskett, 'The Arabic Literature of Nigeria to 1804: a Provisional Note', *Bulletin of the School of Oriental and African Studies*, vol. 25, no. 1, 1962, pp. 135ff.

12. *Ibid.*, p. 137.

13. J. Goody, 'Restricted Literacy in Northern Ghana', p. 235.

14. I want to thank my colleague Simon Ottenberg for generously sharing with me the essence of this interview with Alfa Sawaneh.

15. Personal correspondence, John Hunwick, 16 May 1983.

16. Doutté, *Magie et Religion. . .*, pp. 173–4.

17. Sculptures of *Sowo* commonly exhibit carved Islamic amulets as part of the elegant coiffures that mark this masked spirit. Muslim charms may also be tied to her, however, either to the mask itself or in the raffia costume worn by the dancer. Fred Lamp, associate curator at the Baltimore Museum of Art, kindly sent me a copy of one such amulet which he found in the fibres of a 'Bondo' costume (correspondence dated 11 November, 1982). It is a lengthy amulet and includes the *Ayat al Kursi*, or Throne Verse, praising Allah's immanence; the precise phrase from *Tā Hā* found in Alfa Sawaneh's *yawa dudu*; and three *khawatim* or magical squares containing letters and numbers. The *khawatim* are preceeded by the benediction 'you will be blessed with these *khawatim*, here and in the hereafter'. In His omnipresence, Allah enlarges the very majesty and mystery of *Sowo*.

18. This mask was purchased in 1926 by the Quinn estate for the University Museum, University of Pennsylvania, and was catalogued by H.U. Hall in 1932. Acc. #AF5373.

19. Muhammad Marmaduke Pickthall, *The Glorious Koran*, 2nd edn (Albany: State University of New York Press, 1976) p. 824.

## CHAPTER THREE
## Victory from Allah

1. Phototheque, Musée de L'Homme. Catalog #64-12308-17.

2. I want to thank the staff of the Phototeque, and especially Muguette Dumont, for their courtesy and warm interest during my brief visit to this exceptional archive. My debt of gratitude to other members of the Musée de L'Homme staff extends to Mme Jacqueline N'Diaye, curator of the Arts of Black Africa, and Dominique Champault, of the North African and Near Eastern Department, for their collegiality and their encouragement regarding this project.

3. The best source for the Mahdist movement and British involvement in the Sudan is the detailed study by P.M. Holt, *The Mahdist State in the Sudan 1881–1898* (Oxford: Clarendon Press, 1970).

4. Ignac Goldziher, *Vorlesungen Uber den Islam* (Heidelberg: Carl Winter's Universitatsbuchhandlung, 1910) pp. 22 and 25.

5. I have borrowed the phrase 'sword of truth' from the title of Mervyn Hiskett's excellent book *The*

*Sword of Truth: the Life and Times of the Shehu Usuman dan Fodio* (New York: Oxford University Press, 1973). I am also using Hiskett's wording 'the way of God' in referring to holy war. It comes from his title for ch. 6, 'Holy War in the Way of God', in the same volume.

6. Stanlake Samkange, 'Wars of Resistance', ch. 10 in Alvin M. Josephy Jr. (ed.), *The Horizon History of Africa* (New York: American Heritage Publishing, 1971) p. 410.

7. I want to thank Professors John Hunwick and Farhat Ziadeh for translating the Arabic passages on these flags.

8. F.R. Wingate, *Mahdism and the Egyptian Sudan* (London: Frank Cass, 2nd edn, 1968) pp. 47–8.

9. E.A. Wallis Budge, *Amulets and Talismans* (New York: Macmillan, 1970). Reprint of 1930 edition entitled *Amulets and Superstitions*, pp. 40 and 45. See also E. Doutté, *Magie et Religion dans l'Afrique du Nord* (Algiers: Adolphe Jourdan, 1908) pp. 154ff.

10. This photograph is located in a box of prints entitled Sudan, Ethiopia and Somaliland in the photographic archives of the Museum of Mankind, Burlington Gardens, London.

11. For a similar slit drum, collected among the Azande at the turn of the century and deposited at the British Museum, see C.G. Seligmann 'An Ausumgwa Drum' in *Man*, 1911, 7.

12. *Notable Acquisitions 1975–79*, Metropolitan Museum of Art, 1979, p. 29.

13. *Masterpieces from the Sir Henry Wellcome Collection at U.C.L.A.* (UCLA: Museum of Ethnic Art and Laboratories) p. 6.

14. A.D.H. Bivar, *Nigerian Panoply* (Lagos: 1964) pp. 12–13. I am indebted to Mr Ray Al. Silverman for alerting me to this study.

# CHAPTER FOUR
## Ramadan

1. My research in various Dyula communities in the Ivory Coast and Upper Volta has been conducted at intervals over the last fifteen years. My initial exposure to Ramadan among the Dyula occurred in December 1966 and early January 1967 in the towns of Bondoukou and Bouna in Ivory Coast. I have observed portions of this month among the Dyula of Bobo Dioulasso in October – November 1972 and in June 1982. I wish to express my sincerest thanks to the Foreign Area Fellowship Program and the Social Science Research Council for their generous support of my research.

2. G.E. Von Grunebaum, *Muhammadan Festivals*, p. 56, ch. 3, devoted to Ramadan, is an excellent introduction to the history of this important holiday throughout the Muslim world. For the thoughts of Ghazzali on the subject of the fast and fasting see pp. 56–9.

3. *Ibid*, pp. 57–8.

4. Arthur J. Arberry (translator), *The Koran Interpreted*, Sura 2, verse 183, p. 53.

5. *Ibid*.

6. While *dodo* appears to have originated among the Dyula of Kongbougou it is today undertaken by virtually all Muslim children. Some *dodo* troupes arise even among non-Muslim peoples like the Bobo and immigrant Lobi. On any given night during Ramadan the city of Bobo-Dioulasso is filled with little groups of children carrying out their own versions of *dodo*. Also performed in the capital city of Ouagadougou , since 1972, it has been elaborated into a competitive event at the Peoples' Hall, replete with official judging, entrance fees, elaborate staging and a winner's trophy.

7. M. Prouteaux, 'Divertissements de Kong', *Bulletin du Comité d'Études Historiques et Scientifiques de l'Afrique Occidentale Française* (Dakar: 1925, vol. 8, no. 4) pp. 608–10. L. Quimby, 'Transformations of Belief – Islam among the Dyula of Kongbougou from 1880 to 1970', (Ph.D. dissertation, University of Wisconsin, 1972).

8. Quimby, 'Transformations of Belief', pp. 73–4.

9. Prouteaux, 'Divertissements de Kong', pp. 608–9.

10. Arberry, *The Koran Interpreted*, p. 345.

11. The importance of *Lailat al Kadr* in the life of West African Muslims, especially for Manding peoples such as the Dyula and cultures influenced by Manding civilization, has been noted by Trimmingham: 'A Mande feast of the virgins has been attached to this date. In western Guinea, children sing for presents, young men and maidens parade the streets, singing and dancing all night. They carry around "floats" with representations of animals, boats, and the like'. J.S. Trimmingham, *Islam in West Africa* (Oxford: Clarendon Press, 1959) p. 78.

12. R.A. Bravmann, *Islam and Tribal Art in West Africa* (Cambridge University Press, 1974) pp. 155–6. See also Louis Tauxier, *Le Noir de Bondoukou* (Paris: E. Leroux, 1921) pp. 292–5.

13. Bravmann, *Islam and Tribal Art . . .*, ch. 8, 'The Do Masking Tradition'.

14. Prouteaux, 'Divertissements de Kong', p. 623.

15. *Ibid.*, pp. 624–35.

16. Dr Kathy Green, who carried out historical research in Kong in the late 1970s, confirmed the use of masks among the Dyula at the present time. Discussion with Green, November 1981.

## CHAPTER FIVE
## al-Burāq

1. Lowie Museum of Anthropology, University of California (Berkeley), catalogue # 5-10184.
2. I want to thank Diana de Treville for bringing this print of al-Burāq to my attention and for making available to me her translation (6/8/1974) of its inscriptions. Personal correspondence 22 July, 1975. The sacred and distant mosques mentioned in this verse are thought by Koranic scholars to refer to the sanctuary in Mecca and a sacred place in the highest of the seven heavens. See J. Horovitz' discussion of Miradj in the *Encyclopedia of Islam*, vol. 3, pp. 505–6 (Leiden: E.J. Brill) 1913–36.
3. Translation by de Treville 8/6/1974.
4. For Hausa praises and biographies of the Prophet containing descriptions of al-Burāq see 'Ode in Praise of the Messenger' by Asma bint Shehu (the daughter of Usuman dan Fodio) and the 'Song of Muhamad' by Asim Degel of Sokoto. Mervyn Hiskett, *A History of Hausa Islamic Verse* (London: SOAS, 1975) pp. 44–8 and 53–7. On al-Buraq in Swahili versions of Muhammad's ascension see Jan Knappert, *Traditional Swahili Poetry* (Leiden: E.J. Brill, 1967) pp. 201–5.
5. Horovitz, 'Miradj', p. 505.
6. *Ibid.*, pp. 506–7.
7. *Ibid.*, p. 507.
8. de Treville, Notes on al-Burāq, 8/6/1974.
9. Thomas W. Arnold, *Painting in Islam* (Oxford: Clarendon Press, 1928) p. 120.
10. *Ibid.*, pp. 121–2.
11. Personal communication from Simon Ottenberg 9/7/1983.
12. *Ibid.*
13. I want to thank Dr John W. Nunley for sharing with me his knowledge of Sierra Leone 'Lanterns' and for directing me to Robert Wellesley Cole's charming book *Kossoh Town Boy* (London: Cambridge University Press, 1960).
14. Cole, *Kossoh Town Boy*, p. 124.
15. *Ibid.*, p. 126.
16. This phenomenon of an urban Muslim festival undergoing gradual secularization seems to be paralleled by a similar, and surely related, tradition of illuminated floats in the Senegambia currently being studied by Dr Judith Bettelheim. The festival is known as 'Lanterns' in Gambia and 'Fanal' in Senegal. Although performed at Christmas, this festival may well have its roots in another Muslim procession of floats and lanterns associated with the festival of Tabaski, known as *Id al Kabir* or the great prayer, held on the 12th day of the last month of the Muslim calendar. This is suggested by an illustration of a grand performance held at Tabaski in St Louis, Senegal in 1877 by M. Eugene Blanguernon, a correspondent for the French weekly *Le Journal Illustré*. In Blanguernon's illustration there is a large crowd of Muslims – the women move together clapping and singing; some of the men hold illuminated lanterns shaped like mosques at the end of long poles, others pull two very large floats, one a sailing vessel, the other a mosque, both illuminated by lanterns. Blanguernon's sketch of the Tabaski procession appears in William H. Schneider, *An Empire for the Masses: The French Popular Image of Africa, 1870–1900* (Westport: Greenwood Press, 1982) p. 98. I want to thank Dr Jean Borghatti for alerting me to this fascinating drawing.
17. My information on Islamic themes in Freetown 'Lanterns' comes from J.W. Nunley and a set of slides kindly sent to me by Dr Robin Poyner who photographed this extraordinary spectacle in Freetown on the night of 21/7/1982.
18. My thanks to J.W. Nunley for allowing me to use his excellent slides of this splendid mask of al-Burāq.
19. Musée de l'Homme catalogue # 33.40.90.
20. D.T. Niane, *Le Soudan Occidental Au Temps des Grand Empires* (Paris: Presence Africaine, 19??) plates between pp. 216 and 217. A similar Baga al-Burāq from the collection of the Musée des Arts Africa0ins et Océaniens (catalogue # 64.16.8) appears in the catalogue *Esprits et Dieux d'Afrique* (Musée National, Message Biblique Marc Chagall, Nice) 5 July – 3 November, 1980, (*Editions de la Reunion des Musées Nationaux*) p. 87. I want to thank Mme Colette Noll, curator of African arts at the MAAO for furnishing me with this reference. In this catalogue the work is described as a 'marionette: boat and figures. The figure in the bow represents al-Burāq, winged horse of the prophet Muhammad'.
21. *Ibid.*

## CHAPTER SIX
## Islamic patterns

1. For two relatively recent statements on the legality of representation or *taswir* in Islamic

Art see: Bishr Fares 'De la figuration en Islam: un document inédit', *Arts*, 30 March 1951: 3, and Ahmad Isa 'Muslims and Taswir', in H.W. Glidden, trans., *The Muslim World*, 45 (1955), pp. 250–68.

2.  Oleg Grabar, 'Islamic Art: Art of a Culture or Art of a Faith?', *Art and Archaeology Papers* (AARP) 9, April 1976, p. 3.

3.  Richard Ettinghausen, 'The Man-Made Setting', in Bernard Lewis (ed.), *The World of Islam* (London, Thames and Hudson, 1976) p. 70.

4.  *Ibid.*, p. 72.

5.  *Ibid.*, p. 68.

6.  *Ibid.*, p. 70.

7.  *Ibid.*, p. 59.

8.  *Ibid.*

9.  *Ibid.*, p. 70.

10. Jacob Bronowski, *The Ascent of Man* (Boston: Little, Brown, 1973) p. 166. Bronowski's treatment of the relationships between Arab mathematics and design is elegant and wonderfully clear and is found in chapter 3, 'The Music of the Spheres'.

11. *Ibid.*, p. 172.

12. Oleg Grabar, 'What Makes Islamic Art Islamic?' *AARP* 9, April 1976, p. 2.

13. *Ibid.*

14. *Ibid.*

15. Metropolitan Museum of Art catalog # 1979. 206.279.

16. An excellent study of the Hausa male character is Anthony H.M. Kirk-Greene's *Mutumin-Kirkii – The Concept of the Good Man in Hausa* (Bloomington: Indiana University African Studies Program, 1967).

17. Horace Miner, *The Primitive City of Timbuctoo* (Princeton University Press, 1953) p. 35.

18. *Ibid.*, pp. 34–5.

19. National Museum of African Art catalog # 82-6-2.

20. Museum of the Philadelphia Civic Center catalog # 1894.1.6.

21. Museum of the Philadelphia Civic Center catalog # 1900.1.197.

## CHAPTER SEVEN
### The Swahili coast

1.  Jan Knappert, *Four Centuries of Swahili Verse*, p. xix.

2.  J. de V. Allen, 'Swahili Culture Reconsidered' *Azania*, 9, p. 134.

3.  *Ibid.*

4.  J. de V. Allen, *Lamu*, p. 2.

5.  National Museum of Natural History, Smithsonian Institution, catalog # 409.943.

6.  Allen, 'Swahili Culture Reconsidered', p. 118.

7.  *Ibid.*

8.  Allen, *Lamu*, p. 12.

9.  National Museum of Natural History, Smithsonian Institution catalog # 409.935 (box from Lamu), # 409.947 a, b (lidded bowl from Siyu).

10. Allen, *Lamu*, pp. 9–10.

11. *Ibid.*, p. 10.

12. Nommo Gallery, *Islamic Art*, p. 35.

13. *Ibid.*, p. 47.

# Bibliography

Allen, James de Vere, *Lamu* (Nairobi: Regal Press, N.D.).
————— , 'Swahili Ornament: A Study of the Decoration of the Eighteenth-Century Plasterwork and Carved Doors in the Lamu Region', in *Art and Archaeology Research Papers (AARP)*, vol. 3, June 1973.
————— , 'A Further Note on Swahili Ornament', in *AARP*, vol. 4, Dec. 1973.
————— , 'Swahili Architecture in the Later Middle Ages', *African Arts*, 7 (1974) 2.
————— , 'Swahili Culture Reconsidered', *Azania*, 9, 1974.
————— , and Wilson, T.H., *Swahili Houses and Tombs of the Coast of Kenya* (London 1977).
Arberry, Arthur J., *Sufism* (London: George Allen & Unwin, 1950).
————— , (trans.), *The Koran Interpreted* (New York: MacMillan, 7th printing, 1976).
Arnold, Thomas W., *Painting in Islam* (Oxford: Clarendon Press, 1928).
*Art Nègre*, Sources, Evolution, Expansion (Dakar-Paris, catalogue, 1966).
*Arts Africains*, Musée Cantini, 1970 (catalogue).
Arts Council of Great Britain, *The Arts of Islam* (Catalogue of the Festival of Islam), London, 1976.

Bivar, A.D.H. and Hiskett, M., 'The Arabic Literature of Nigeria to 1804: A Provisional Account', *Bulletin of the School of Oriental and African Studies*, 25, Part 1 (1962).

Bivar, A.D.H., *Nigerian Panoply* (Lagos: 1964).

Bravmann, René A., *Islam and Tribal Art in West Africa* (Cambridge University Press, 1974).

Bronowski, J., *The Ascent of Man* (Boston: Little, Brown, 1973).

Budge, E.A. Wallis, *Amulets and Talismans* (New York: Macmillan, 1970).

Cohen, Abner, *Custom and Politics in Urban Africa* (Berkeley: University of California Press, 1969).

Cole, Robert Wellesley, *Kossoh Town Boy* (London: Cambridge University Press, 1960).

Cruise O'Brien, D.B., *The Mourides of Senegal* (Oxford: Clarendon Press, 1971).

Doutté, Edmond, *Les Marabouts* (Paris: Leroux, 1900).

——————— , *Magie et Religion dans l'Afrique du Nord* (Algiers: Adolphe Jourdan, 1908).

Ettinghausen, Richard, 'The Character of Islamic Art', in Nabih A. Faris (ed.), *The Arab Heritage* (Princeton: University Press, 1944).

——————— , 'Interaction and Integration in Islamic Art', in G.E. von Grunebaum (ed.), *Unity and Variety in Muslim Civilization* (Chicago: University Press, 1955).

——————— , 'The Man-Made Setting', in Bernard Lewis (ed.), *The World of Islam* (London: Thames & Hudson, 1976).

Fares, Bishr, 'De la figuration en Islam: un document inédit', *Arts*, 3, 30 March 1951.

Gabus, Jean, *Au Sahara*, 2 vols. (Neuchatel: Editions de la Baconnière, 1955 and 1958).

Gaudefroy-Demombynes, Maurice, *Muslim Institutions*, trans. John P. MacGregor (London: George Allen & Unwin, 1950).

Geertz, Clifford, 'Art as a Cultural System', *Modern Language Notes*, vol. 91, 1976.

Goldziher, Ignac, *Vorlesungen Uber den Islam* (Heidelberg: Universitatsbuchandlung, 1910).

Goody, J.R. (ed.), *Literacy in Traditional Societies* (Cambridge University Press, 1968).

——————— , 'Restricted Literacy in Northern Ghana', in J.R. Goody (ed.), *Literacy in Traditional Societies* (Cambridge University Press, 1968).

Grabar, Oleg, *The Formation of Islamic Art* (New Haven: Yale University, 1973).

——————— , 'What Makes Islamic Art Islamic?', *AARP*, 9, April 1976.

——————— , 'Islamic Art: Art of a Culture or Art of a Faith?' in *AARP*, 13, June 1978.

Greenberg, Joseph Harold, *The Influence of Islam on a Sudanese Religion* (New York: J.J. Augustin, 1947).

Grottanelli, V.L., 'Somali Wood Engravings', in *African Arts*, 1, 3 (1968).

Hiskett, Mervyn, *A History of Hausa Islamic Verse* (London: School of Oriental and African Studies, 1975).

——————— , *The Sword of Truth: The Life and Times of the Shehu Usuman dan Fodio* (New York: Oxford University Press, 1973).

Holt, P.M., *The Mahdist State in the Sudan, 1881–1898* (Oxford: Clarendon Press, 1970).

Horovitz, J., 'Miradj' in *Encyclopedia of Islam* (old edn.) (Leiden: E.J. Brill, 1913–36).

Hunwick, John O., *Islam and Africa: Friend or Foe* (Accra: Ghana Universities Press, 1976).

Isa, Ahmad, 'Muslims and Taswir', in H.W. Glidden (trans.), *The Muslim World*, 45, 1955, pp. 250–68.

*Islamic Arts* (Nairobi: Nommo Gallery, 1969). Essay by J.D.V. Allen.

Kirk-Greene, Anthony H.M., *Mutumin Kirkii – The Concept of the Good Man in Hausa* (Bloomington: Indiana University African Studies Program, 1974).

Knappert, Jan, *Traditional Swahili Poetry* (Leiden: E.J. Brill, 1967).

——————— , *Four Centuries of Swahili Verse* (London: Heinemann, 1979).

Lane, Edward William, *An Account of the Manners and Customs of the Ancient Egyptians* (London: East-West Publications, 1978 reprint of the 1895 edition).

Levtzion, Nehemiah, *Muslims and Chiefs in West Africa* (Oxford: Clarendon Press, 1968).

Lewis, Bernard (ed.), *The World of Islam* (London: Thames & Hudson, 1976).

Lewis, I.M. (ed.), *Islam in Tropical Africa* (London: Oxford University Press for the International African Institute, 1966).

Martin, B.G., *Muslim Brotherhoods in Nineteenth-Century Africa* (Cambridge University Press, 1976).

Marty, Paul, *L'Islam en Guinée: Fouta Diallon* (Paris: E. Leroux, 1921).

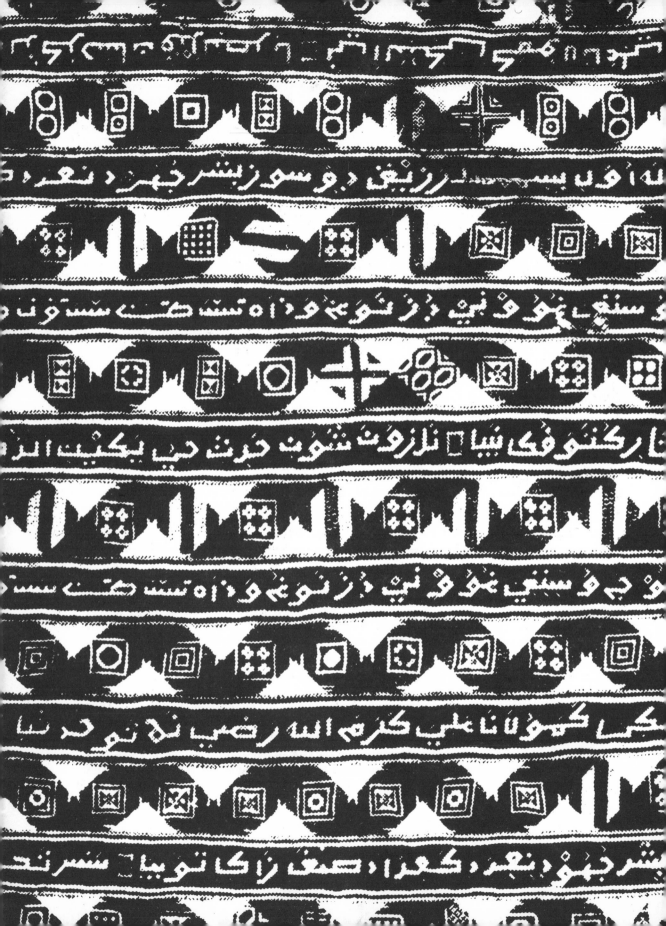